My Child, My Disciple

My Child,

Edited by Sarah Shapiro

Jerusalem / New York

My Disciple

A Practical, Torah-Based Guide to
Effective Discipline in the Home

by Rabbi Noach Orlowek

With Foreword by HaRav HaGaon
Rav Simcha Wasserman *zt"l*

FELDHEIM *Publishers*

© Copyright 1993 by
Rabbi N. Orlowek, POB 1570 Jerusalem, Israel.

All rights reserved. No part of this publication may be translated, dramatized, reproduced, stored in a retrieval system or transmitted, **in any form** or by any means, electronic, mechanical, photocopying, recording or otherwise, without prior permission in writing from the publishers. Printed in Israel. The rights of the copyright holder will be strictly enforced.

Typeset by *Dagush* International, Ma'ale Amos, Israel.

Library of Congress Cataloging-in-Publication Data

Orlowek, Noach.
    My child, my disciple; a practical, Torah-based guide to effective discipline in the home / by Noach Orlowek; with foreword by Simcha Wasserman.
       p.   cm.
    Includes bibliographical references.
    ISBN 0-87306-645-6
    1. Discipline of children—Religious aspects—Judaism. 2. Jewish families. I. Title.
BM727.075 1994
649.64—dc20   93-46947

10 9 8 7 6 5 4

Distributed by:
FELDHEIM PUBLISHERS   J. LEHMANN Hebrew Booksellers
200 Airport Executive Park   20 Cambridge Terrace
Nanuet, New York 10954   Gateshead, Tyne & Wear

Printed in Israel

In Memory of Our Beloved Parents

לעילוי נשמת

דוד בן זכיה

נ.ל.ב.ע. ג' טבת תשנ"ב

ולעילוי נשמת

אליאן בת פרידה

נ.ל.ב.ע. ה' סיון תשל"ט

ת.נ.צ.ב.ה.

David G. & Eliane Sassoon

זכרונם לברכה

Whose love for family, Torah and Jewish identity
gave them the strength to raise
a proud Jewish family in far-off Japan.

Rav Pinchos Weiner, *zt"l*, was a *mechanech par excellence*, caring deeply about all aspects of his students' growth and well-being, understanding their needs and helping them achieve their highest potential.
He was a *medakdek b'mitzvos*, קלה כחומרה.
He was the person that gave the author his first chance at teaching elementary school. He taught me, encouraged me, and, above all, believed in me.
My debt to him is irrepayable.

לעילוי נשמת
הרב פנחס ניסן זצ"ל
בן הרב מרדכי זצ"ל
נלב"ע י"ט כסלו תשנ"ה
ת.נ.צ.ב.ה.

Approbation from *Mori VeRabi* HaRav HaGaon
Rabbi Chaim P. Scheinberg, *Shlita*

Rabbi CHAIM P. SCHEINBERG
Rosh Hayeshiva "TORAH-ORE"
and Morah Hora'ah of Kiryat Mattersdorf

הרב חיים פינחס שיינברג
ראש ישיבת "תורה-אור"
ומורה הוראה דקרית מטרסדורף
בס״ד

בס״ד

ירושלים, י״ט אדר תשנ״ג

    Disciplining children, both in the home and at school, is a challenging task for even the most capable parent or teacher. It is, to paraphrase our Sages, (שבת קיז) חכמה ואינה מלאכה, the result of much thought and wisdom. Parents and teachers invest a good deal of effort in discipline, yet often with poor results. This is because they lack guidance in understanding how and why children can be taught to gladly accept the direction offered by their teachers or parents.

    Rav Noach Orlowek, *shlita*, has been well-known in Yerushalayim for many years for the successful guidance he gives to parents and teachers. His own rich experience, combined with his closeness to some of our generation's great *mechanchim* has helped him formulate practical Torah-based solutions for the varied and often complicated problems that are brought to his attention.

    May his new books, "*My Child, My Disciple*," which deals with discipline at home, and "*My Disciple, My Child*," which offers practical insights into classroom discipline, avail this הדרכה to a much wider audience, both in ארץ ישראל and in חוץ לארץ.

רחוב פנים מאירות 2, ירושלים, ת. ד. 6979, טל. 371513-(02), ישראל
2, Panim Meirot St., Jerusalem, P. O. B. 6979, Tel (02)-371513, Israel

בירת המוסר

ע"ש ר' חיים מנחם להמן ע"ה
רח' הרב סורוצקין 39 ירושלים
מיסודו של תנועת שוחרי מוסר, ירושלים

Institute for Torah Ethics
IN MEMORY OF R'CHAIM MENACHEM LEHMANN
39 Harav Sorotzkin St., Jerusalem

בס"ד

Approbation from HaRav HaGaon Rabbi Shlomo Wolbe, *Shlita*

כ"ב אדר תשנ"ג

הי"כ
ידידי הנעלה הגדול בתורה ובחכמת היראה איש בר לבב
ורב תבונות מוהר"ר נח אורלווק שליט"א
אחד"ש כתרוו"ט באהבה והוקרה רבה!

שמחתי לשמוע שכת"ר עומד להוציא לאור שני ספרים, אחד להדרכת הורים ואחד להדרכת מורים. הן כת"ר הוא האיש המסוגל לפתוח השער לחכמת-חינוך העמוקה, בנסיונו הרב עם תלמידים צעירים ומבוגרים, אשר בטוהר לבו ידע תמיד לגשת אל לב תלמידיו לקרבם ולאהב עליהם לימוד תורה וקיום המצוות.

אין ספק כי רבים ימצאו בספרי כת"ר את המסלולים האמיתיים ללב בניהם ותלמידיהם ותרבה הדעת בחכמת החינוך. אם תמיד היה החינוך עבודה קשה, היום היא קשה שבעתיים, הן מצד ירידת הדור בדעת והשקיעה בשטחיות, והן בעקבות המתירנות וההפקרות המשתוללת באין מעצור.

יישר כח כת"ר, ויענהו השי"ת להמשיך בעבודתו הברוכה ברוב הצלחה ויהיה מהמזכים את הרבים ככוכבים לעולם ועד.

כעתירת ידיד מוקירו ומכבדו כרום ערכו

שלמה וולבה

Approbation from HaRav HaGaon Rabbi Nachman Bulman, *Shlita*

KIRYAT NACHLIEL · קרית נחליאל

RABBI NACHMAN BULMAN — הרב נחמן בולמן

בס״ד

בס״ד   ה׳ טבת תשנ״ג

There is a tightrope to be walked by Torah-educators: transmission of a sacred heritage and/or development of individual personality; discipline vs. self-motivation; 'molding' the child, or understanding and cultivating the child's makeup and inclinations; an authoritarian approval, or a voluntaristic one.

R. Israel Salanter used to say that the matter is akin to holding a bird in hand, if one holds the bird even a bit too tightly, it chokes. If one holds the bird even a bit too lightly, it flies away.

R. Noach Orlowek is a noted Torah-educator with rich experience and depth of insight. After much oral teaching — to both teachers and parents — he has authored two books which offer guidance to parents and educators respectively. One is entitled: *"My Child, My Disciple."* The other is named: *"My Disciple, My Child."*

Together, the work is a beautiful unity, which blends a rich texture of Torah sources with sensitive guidance. In our times of generation gaps, the appearance of R. Orlowek's work can serve to fulfill a vital need.

It is the hope of the undersigned that many — parents and teachers — will benefit from R. Orlowek's insight and dedication.

הכותב לכבוד התורה לומדי׳ ומלמדי׳ לילדי עם התורה,

נחמן בולמן

Acknowledgments

If not for my dear friend Rav Zelig Pliskin, *shlita*, this book would simply not exist. Originally, I had intended to write only a teachers' manual. But Rav Zelig insisted that I write a parenting book to go along with *My Disciple, My Child*, which was designed primarily with teachers and educators in mind. He also took the time to read both books and offer his insightful comments. To him I express my deepest gratitude, and I thank Hashem for giving me the privilege of knowing him.

I am indebted to HaGaon Rav Nachman Bulman, *shlita*, who took time from his busy schedule to read both *My Child, My Disciple* and *My Disciple, My Child* and unstintingly shared with me his wisdom, gleaned from decades of serving *Klal Yisroel*.

Mrs. Sarah Shapiro graced these books not only with her editorial skills, but with her heart and soul. The titles were her idea, reflecting her understanding of and commitment to the ideals expressed in these books.

Several mothers took time to read parts of the manuscript and reassured me that the points were indeed clear. Among them were Mrs. Brocha Parkoff, Mrs. Nechama Berg, Mrs.

Esther Abramov, and Mrs. Yitti Bisk. Their encouragement was vital, for this volume is intended primarily to provide *practical* and *understandable* insights into the root causes of disciplinary problems.

Reb Noach and Donna Greenberg of Tsfas graciously enabled me to have many days of peace and quiet in their home — and it was there that this book had its genesis. Reb Dovid and Miriam Grossman helped with this book in many and varied ways. Their uncommon common sense and gracious character are rare indeed.

Rav Chaim Septimus, *shlita*, Rav Dovid Rossoff, *shlita*, Rav Yisroel Fabian, *shlita*, and Rav Yehuda Mendelsohn, *shlita*, had insightful comments, as did Rav Eli Gewirtz, *shlita*, director of the Parent Enrichment Program of Torah Umesorah.

Rav Hanoch Teller, *shlita*, a dear friend and colleague, was instrumental in bringing me into contact with the fine professionals who gave both *My Child, My Disciple* and *My Disciple, My Child* their final format. These include Reb Yaakov Feldheim and his staff, Ben Gasner, and Yechiel and Tybi Kapiloff, of *Dagush* International Typesetters. I am grateful to Mrs. Fern Seckbach who gave this book its final proofeading.

My dear father, Mr. Sidney Orlowek, may he be well, always has been a role model for me, inculcating in his children many of the ideas expressed in this book. May he derive *nachas* from this work, and from his children, grandchildren, and great-grandchildren. This book is also a tribute to my mother, Esther *bas* Yehoshua Ephraim, *o"h*, who dedicated herself to and sacrificed for the Torah education of her children. It can truly be said of her, "*Sheli veshelcha sheloh he,*" whatever benefit is gleaned from this work is in her merit.

My brother Dovid has taught me many things, but most of all he taught me, by example, of the inestimable importance of having a rebbe. May he and my brother Michael have much *nachas* from their families.

My dear parents-in-law, Rabbi and Mrs. Solomon Freilich of Mount Vernon, New York, have treated me like a son. They have been at my side in all my endeavors for the past twenty-two years. May they have much *nachas* from their sons, Rav Yehoshua and Rav Akiva, from their daughter Rena and myself, and from our families.

Last but certainly not least, my wife, Rena, deserves my deepest thanks for more than I can ever say. May we share much *siyata dishmaya* in raising our children to bring *nachas* to their Creator.

Rabbi Noach Orlowek
February 21st 1993
Yerushalayim, ת״ו

A Humble Tribute and Dedication

to

Mori VeRabi

HaGaon Rav Simcha Wasserman

and to

HaRabbanis Moras

Feige Rochel Wasserman

zichronum livrocha

On the second of Cheshvon 5753 we lost *Mori VeRabi*, HaGaon Rav Simcha Wasserman, *zt"l*,[1] and ten days later we

---

1. Many knew him simply as Rebbe. Others referred to him as "the Rosh Yeshiva." In this Tribute, we will use the title with which the author is accustomed, Rebbe.

lost the Rebbetzen, *o"h*. The pain is still too fresh to properly speak about this blow to the Jewish people, but for myself I somehow feel that I will never be able to accurately evaluate neither the merit I had in being Rebbe's *talmid* nor the magnitude of my loss. I feel like an infant orphaned by his illustrious father, who lacks the wherewithal to comprehend what has happened to him.

Rebbe, *zt"l*, expressed his life credo in his will. He permitted *one* eulogizer[2] to mention that during Rebbe's lifetime he undertook to teach students according to their ability to understand. For Rebbe taught Torah only for the benefit of his student, this being one of the paramount ways that Rebbe gave of himself to those around him. He used to say in the name of his illustrious father, Reb Elchonon, may Hashem avenge his blood, that the greatest kindliness that man can do in this world is to study Torah. Rebbe always mentioned that according to the Rambam the *teaching* of Torah is an integral part of *studying* Torah. Rebbe was willing, and eminently able, to bestow this kindliness upon everyone.

Rebbe was a giver and his life's message was that only givers can be truly happy and serve Hashem properly. He was fond of repeating that Eretz Yisroel has two Seas. One, the Sea of Galilee, is vibrant and alive. It is a giver, feeding and invigorating the Land. The other Sea is only a taker, and is therefore called the Dead Sea. He took nothing for himself, and until his last days thought only what he could do for others, as the following aptly demonstrates.

Dr. Howard Lebowitz had the privilege of being close to Rebbe during his final days at Brigham and Womens Hos-

---

2. And then only if the Rebbetzen would outlive him and be present at the funeral. In the event that she was to depart this world before him, Rebbe forbade any eulogies.

pital in Boston. He told me afterwards that the intensive care unit personnel said they realized what a great man was in their care when it became apparent that his chief concern was the welfare of his visitors. They felt that this was an amazing attitude for someone in critical condition.

They were amazed, but in truth it was the fruit of a lifetime of selflessness. This had become Rebbe's essence and hence remained an integral part of his character under the most trying situations.

Rav Hillel Zaks, shlita, rosh yeshiva of Chevron Yeshiva in Yerushalayim, recalls when he was invited to give a lecture at Rebbe's yeshiva in Los Angeles. Shortly before Rav Hillel was to leave his lodging, Rebbe called to say that he would not be able to attend, but that the lecture should continue as scheduled. The line then went dead. Only later did Rav Zaks learn that Rebbe had just suffered a heart attack and that he had called Rav Zaks with the consent of the ambulance attendant. Rebbe was concerned that Rebbe's absence might worry Rav Hillel. After he had delivered his message, the paramedic hung up the phone and put him on a respirator — but not before Rebbe had instructed the Rebbetzen to be present when Rav Hillel came to the yeshiva, lest he be concerned about her absence as well.

Another story puts this point into the sharpest possible focus.

Boruch Levine, who was present at the time of Rebbe's passing, tells us something that has been known to occur only rarely and with the greatest of men. Boruch, in attendance at the I.C.U. of Brookdale Hospital in Brooklyn, upon seeing what was happening, began to break down. Rebbe, seeing Boruch's state of mind, **spent the last moments of his life comforting him**.

We cannot even begin to evaluate our loss.

The Rebbetzen, *o"h*, was also a paragon giver. I often witnessed her joy in being of help to others. At the *shiva* for Rebbe I saw with my own eyes how she made sure that a certain unmarried young man would get assistance in helping find his life partner — this at a time when we can only guess at the pain she was enduring. She had told me after returning home from the funeral that "He was an angel; when he entered the house, the house lit up." Saturday night after the *shiva* (which had ended on the previous Friday) she remarked to Rav Shlomo Lorincz that she hadn't thought she could live without Rebbe. Several hours later she was gone.

The Rebbe and the Rebbetzen were there for others, never asking for themselves. They were truly מזכי הרבים, those who bring merit to the community, who are compared to stars which shine eternally (Doniel 12:3). Rebbe explained this as follows:

> *Stars are hundreds of light years away from Earth. This means that even after a star has ceased to emanate light, its twinkle will still be seen in the heavens for centuries to come. So too does the merit of those who bring merit to the community continues to shine, long after they themselves have ceased to shine.*

Without a doubt, this applies to the Rebbe and Rebbetzen.

The *Ohr Yoheil*, written by the Gaon Rav Leib Chasman, *zt"l* (*mashgiach* of Chevron Yeshiva in Yerushalayim), states that a *talmid* who truly loves his rebbe should see to it that his rebbe's investment in his student has not been in vain (*Shvivei Ohr*, p.177).

Rebbe saw the various stages of this book and approved every quotation attributed to him.[3] In particular, the foreword is the result of a session especially recorded for this purpose and, following several sessions where the wording of the tape's contents were carefully screened, he approved the written rendition. I had wanted that he see the final fruition of this book, but the *Ribono Shel Olom*, in His infinite wisdom and to our great sorrow, willed otherwise.

Rebbe drew me close to him when I was a thirteen-year-old child and continued to mold me for more than three decades, as he molded so many others, leaving each of us feeling that he was Rebbe's child. I hope and pray that I will give him *nachas*, that his investment in me will, with Hashem's help, bear fruit, and that I will prove worthy of all the time, heart, and soul he so lavishly bestowed upon me.

I humbly urge Rebbe's children all over the world to organize to continue studying Mishnayos each year for him (Elozor Simcha *ben* Elchonon Bunim) and for the Rebbetzen, (Feige Rochel *bas* Meir) as Rebbe specifically requested in his will. Persons willing to accept the responsibility of studying a given *mesechta* can contact me at my mailing address. I will determine what *mesechtos* are available and will be able to suggest to those flexible enough which *mesechtos* should be studied in the coming year.

My mailing address is:
Rabbi N. Orlowek
Box 1570
Jerusalem,
Israel

May Hashem bind the wounds of His nation and bring us His Redeemer speedily in our days.

---

3. Except for the passage on page 57.

An Important Message to the Reader

It has been said in the name of HaGaon Rav Yaakov Kamenetsky, *zt"l*, that there is no *Shulchan Oruch* on the laws of parenting because each situation is unique, so only the parent who is experiencing any specific circumstance can — after consulting those more experienced than he — determine the correct response.

Ultimately, only a parent can make the right decisions regarding his child. Undoubtedly, certain mothers and fathers flagrantly and consistently mishandle their children, but these parents are the exception, not the rule. When confronted by a disciplinary problem, parents are often confused as to which course of action to take. This confusion is frequently rooted in the fact that they don't know how the problem developed. *The primary function of this book is therefore to help parents trace a problem back to its source.* While they can't turn back the clock, the knowledge of how a disciplinary problem began clarifies how it may be rectified.

Parents must realize that so much of what they do is *right*. The fact that you are even reading (or considering reading) this book confirms your commitment to proper parenting. *Don't sell yourself short.*

I would ask even those parents who are not grade-school teachers to read this book's companion volume, *My Disciple, My Child*. HaGaon Rav Yitzchok Hutner, *zt"l*, called a rebbe a "במקום טאטען," a substitute father;[1] many principles mentioned in *My Disciple, My Child* are thus easily applicable to the home. Many are also mentioned in this book, of course, but their classroom application helps concretize them. In addition, reading the teacher's volume may enable you to better understand the trials and tribulations of every teacher and to extend whatever assistance you can.

Reading this book is another way of guarding the *neshoma* or *neshomos* Hashem has entrusted to us. But in the final analysis, only He can truly help us, and to Him we must turn in order to succeed.

---

1. See *Pachad Yitzchok, Shavuos*, at the end of p. 241.

Foreword:

Mori VeRabi
HaGaon Rav Simcha Wasserman *zt"l*

An important life rule to remember is that a person can never be successful if he has more than one aim in what he is doing. It follows that if you want to succeed when teaching a *talmid*, you cannot have one aim for the *talmid* while having your own interests in mind, as well. (This seems to be the reason that it is forbidden to teach Torah for remuneration. When teaching *bechinam* — without pay[1] — then the very act of teaching is solely for the benefit of the *talmid*.)

Chazal[2] tell us that *talmidim* are called their teacher's children. It would seem that any teacher training must therefore be of secondary importance, for if it were of primary importance, then every parent would have to undergo a special training program.

The Rambam states:[3]

> *"Just as a man is obligated to teach his son, so too is he obligated to teach his grandson, as it says:*[4] *'And you shall*

---

1. *Nedorim* 37a.
2. *Sifri*, Devorim 6:7.
3. See Rambam, *Hilchos Talmud Torah* 1:2.
4. Devorim 4:9.

make them [the words of Torah] known to your children and grandchildren.' Not only to his son and grandson, but it is a mitzva for every Jewish scholar to teach all students, even if they are not his sons, as it says,[5] 'And you shall teach them [the words of Torah] to your sons' [and it has been taught] by the Oral Tradition[6] that 'your sons' refer to your talmidim, for talmidim are called 'sons,' as it says:[7] 'And the sons [i.e., students of] the Prophets went forth.'"

The Rambam seems difficult to understand. If a *talmid* is only called a son after being taught, how can the Rambam use the *posuk* of "*Veshinantom levonecho* — and you shall teach to your children" as a source to obligate a scholar to begin teaching? It must mean that the Rambam understands that the posuk is indicating an obligation to *make him your son.*

In truth, however, another point can be made. *Unless he is my son, I cannot teach him.* "*Veshinantom levonecho — eilu hatalmidim*" is because the teaching is always with your son, it follows that *you cannot teach him until you adopt him.*

---

5. Devorim 6:7.
6. Sifri ibid. It seems that the Sifri is referring to a Rabbinic obligation, a חיוב דרבנן. This was what R. Yehoshua Ben Gamla instituted when he set up the system of formal education for the young; that the scholar became *obligated* to "adopt" the child of a father who could not teach his son Torah and to make that child his own son.

עיין קובץ שיעורים, בבא בתרא כא. "מי שאין לו אב לא היה לומד דכתיב ולמדתם אתם׳, וקשה הא כתיב ושננתם לבניך אלו התלמידים שקרויים בנים, וי״ל דודאי בשעה שכבר הוא תלמידו מיקרי בנו, אבל כל זמן שלא למד לפניו עדיין אינו בנו ואינו חייב לעשותו שיהא בנו."

7. Melochim II 2:3.

So making him your son is part of the mitzva of *"Veshinantom."*

If your son enters the kitchen Friday afternoon while you are preparing a *cholent* and you tell him to leave because he is disturbing you, this is anti-educational. A parent should be concerned only with how his child develops. It would be good chinuch to send him out of the kitchen so as to teach him to avoid being a nuisance to others when they are busy, rather than to do so for the parent's own convenience.

"Ben chacham yisamach av — A wise son will cause his father to rejoice."[8] This is not to be misconstrued as a double aim — the son's wisdom and the father's happiness. Rather, the *nachas* that the father enjoys is an outgrowth of his child's development. But, on the other hand, if a father teaches his child because he wants to have *nachas* from him, the result will be imperfect. When he teaches his child because he wants the child to mature into a correct person, the *nachas* comes as a matter of course.

This is the foundation of all *chinuch*: The *talmid*'s welfare is my only concern. In this way, and *only is this way*, does my *talmid* become my son and my son my *talmid*.

---

8. Mishlei 10:1.

Contents

1. Disciple — Discipline   31
2. Building Life-Long Relationships   35
3. Two Enemies — Surprise & Laziness   45
4. Fair, Firm, and Friendly   51
5. When Parents Disagree   55
6. Honoring Parents — A חוק   59
7. Making Yourself Understood —
   Before a Problem Arises   63
8. Making Yourself Understood — Afterwards   71
9. Time It Right   83
10. Responding Right   87
11. Who Are *You*?   91
12. Always Finding Fault?   97
13. Staying Afloat   103
14. Letting Go   111
15. Watching Your Health   119
16. Reward and Punishment   123
17. How It Looks Doesn't Matter   137
18. Keeping Your Cool   141

Afterword   149
Glossary   151

Note:
Wherever the words
"*Mori VeRabi*" ("my mentor and my teacher") appear
they refer to *Mori VeRabi*
HaGaon Rav Simcha Wasserman, *zt"l*

1

"Disciple — Discipline"

My father taught me that the word "discipline" derives from the word "disciple." For a disciple's learning cannot be forced but must result from the student's *desire* to learn. Likewise, true discipline stems from a desire to follow. As the *Gra*[1] writes, "Learning is retained only through gentleness."[2]

Rav Yitzchok Hutner, *zt"l*,[3] notes[4] that just as the ears hear by detecting sound waves and the eyes see by responding to light waves, the mind also has its medium: *pleasure*. The mind learns what it *wants* to learn, what it enjoys learning. Hence,

---

1. The Vilna Gaon, (1720-1797). He is known by the acronym "Gra," which stands for HaGaon Rabbeinu Eliyahu.
2. See *Iggeres HaGra*: "כי הלימוד אינו נקבע באדם, כי אם בישוב ונחת..."
3. Rav Hutner (1906-1981) was *rosh yeshiva* of Yeshivas Rabbeinu Chaim Berlin and one of America's foremost disseminators of Torah. An ingenious *mechanech*, he plumbed the deepest recesses of his students' souls, molding each *talmid* according to that *talmid*'s unique capabilities.
4. *Pachad Yitzchok, Shavuos, maamar* 15:6.

our Sages tell us that a person should study subjects which he finds pleasurable.[5] For this reason, the blessing said before beginning the day's Torah studies contains the request "And sweeten the words of Your Torah in our mouths...." This principle is as true of discipline as it is of developing a disciple.

"Discipline" rooted in intimidation will evaporate as soon as the disciple is freed — or frees himself — of his fears. Then, enmity and rebellion often surface, with the "disciple" defying even the simplest and most reasonable requests.

In contrast to intimidation, Rashi tells us that when the Torah says to "take" a person, it refers to *convincing* him "with beautiful words!"[6]

Furthermore, the *"Alter,"* Reb Simcha Ziesel Zeev, *zt"l*,[7] writes:

> A student must know two things about his teacher which will inspire him to accept his lessons joyfully and willingly: (1) His teacher is wiser than he and knows better than he what is to [the student's] benefit. (2) His teacher *very* much [emphasis mine] seeks his [student's] good and not his own, *and has no other intention* [emphasis mine].[8]

With regard to parents, the *Alter*[9] adds that a child fails to love his father totally because "he thinks his father does not know what is to his [child's] benefit."

---

5. *Avodah Zorah* 19a. See also Rabbeinu Yona on Mishlei 2:4.
6. See Rashi on Bereishis 2:15, Bemidbar 27:18,22 and Devorim 1:15. Also see *Kiddushin* 22b.
7. Rav Simcha Ziesel Zeev (1824-1898), a major disciple of Rav Yisroel Salanter (1810-1883), is known in the Torah world as the *"Alter* of Kelm," Kelm being the city where he established his famous school.
8. *Chochmah U'Mussar*, vol. 2, *maamar* 225.
9. Ibid.

Sometimes this perception leads to even more than a lack of love. Today, there is a worldwide malady known as the "generation gap." Children feel estranged from their parents. Sometimes children are pushed into a prestigious career because the parents themselves crave prestige. As *Mori VeRabi, zt"l,* said, "'My son the doctor' is the cause of the 'generation gap.'" When a child feels that his parents' expectations, advice, and direction reflect their best interest, rather than his, parent-child communication suffers severely, and far more than discipline is lost.

On the other hand, if parents convey to their child that they have only his best interest at heart, love and respect for them will continue growing as he matures. For example, when non-observant parents enroll their child in a Torah-oriented school simply because they want the most beneficial type of education for him, they need not fear that his studies there will diminish from his respect for them. If anything, the child will find himself thinking, "My parents care about me and want the best for me. They understand life and people and are worth turning to for guidance."

In Summary

- Discipline is rooted in a child's desire to follow his parents' lead because he knows they love him, want what is best for him, and have the good judgment to direct him toward success. **Laying the groundwork for this type of relationship, and pinpointing and dealing with the obstacles to its development, is the key to discipline.**

2

Building Life-Long Relationships

The Hebrew word for "preparation," הכנה, is rooted in the word כַּן – base, for preparation means creating a stable foundation, without which nothing endures.[1]

Going one step farther, the *Avnei Nezer*[2] tell us that the benefit of anything we do is commensurate with our preparation for it.[3] Accordingly, the more we value something, the more extensive our preparation must be.

Preparation takes patience, and "results" usually come

---

1. The word כווּן, direction, also derives from the word כן, base, for the basis of your destination is the direction you take at the outset. כוונה, intent, is spelled similarly, for G-d judges our actions based upon our *intent*.
2. Rav Avrohom Bornstein (1839-1910), the Sochatchover Rebbe.
3. To quote the *Shem MiShemuel*, Devorim, p. 102: "...As my father, זצללה״ה, said, just as Shabbos preparation lasts for three days, for this entire period is considered "before Shabbos," so too does the radiance of the sanctity of Shabbos lingers for three days after Shabbos."

slowly.[4] Laying the groundwork for proper *discipline* consists of nothing less than turning your child into your *disciple*; such an undertaking demands all the patience, care, and insight that you have at your disposal.

The following story demonstrates how highly Judaism values the education of a child:

> *The Russian education minister, Ovarov, once asked Rav Chaim Volozhiner*[5] *when a Jewish child's education begins. He answered, "Twenty years before he is born."*

Rav Chaim expressed a great truth: To succeed with our children, one of life's most important "projects," we must first *build our own character*. This self-development is perhaps the essence of preparation for successful childrearing.

Furthermore, parents must devote time and energy in order to build a proper relationship with their children well before questions of discipline arise. Punishment is usually unnecessary when the parent-child relationship over the long

---

4. In his commentary on Mishlei 9:10, the Vilna Gaon explains that sometimes you must go first in the *opposite direction* of your goal. For example, the *Gemora* (*Brochos* 61a) states that G-d had initially intended to create two people, male and female, but instead created one person and then separated some flesh from the male in order to create a female. G-d certainly hadn't changed His mind. Rather, since His *goal* was to produce two individuals who would function as a unit but separately, first He created the unit and then separated it into two parts. Thus, we, too, must sometimes take a few steps backward before moving forward. If we patiently invest our time and mind and heart, not expecting immediate results, Hashem will help us.
5. Rav Chaim Volozhiner (1749-1821) was the Vilna Gaon's prized pupil, and he founded, in Volozhin, the first yeshiva as we know it in modern times.

term has been basically one of warmth and respect.

Yet it is hard to make your children your disciples because they see you at your weak moments, when exhaustion or frustration have left you frazzled. They see you in your pajamas, at the breakfast table, etc. You lack the idealized aura surrounding their teachers. Although this is as it should be, for parents need to be close to their children, this closeness can make discipline difficult.

Your Edge as a Parent

Nevertheless, as a parent, you have an edge over a teacher, and it is your best hope of making your children your disciples. What is this edge? *Love, time* and *resources.*

Parents have — or *should have* — time for their children, *time to listen.* There is almost no better way to foster a beautiful relationship with your child than to listen attentively to him. When you listen to someone — anyone — he feels cared for and understood. This feeling is no small advantage when you want to get your own points across. Someone who feels loved, heard, and understood is inclined to heed your words. He may not accept your view, but he will certainly give it due respect and consideration.

I think the following statement captures the essence of love: "If it's important to you, it's important to me." When your three-year-old daughter flies through the door and babbles excitedly about the earthshaking incident that took place in nursery school that day, *take time out to listen, for her world was indeed shaken. Don't tell her you're busy. Listen. It's important to her!* If you can't listen right then, set up a time for it later on — *but do it.* Granted, your child must realize that you cannot listen all day long — but make time to hear what's important to her. As for the second factor — resources, parents can offer far better behavioral incentives than teachers. Even parents with limited resources can usually come up with a bigger incentive than a teacher can in a classroom situation.

There is another extremely important thing for parents to remember: *Children want to love and respect their parents.* I have often counseled children who, despite parental mistreatment (real or imagined), wanted to respect and love their parents. We all know that our love for our children is inviolate; yet we tend to forget that a child's love for his parents, while not necessarily as intense as parental love, is also natural and an important part of his self-image. So remember: The *Ribono Shel Olom* imbues both parents and children with love for one another. Even when the going gets rough, we mustn't think we have no bond with our children. We are far likelier to succeed than we think.

In summation, we have the love, time, and resources to help our children far more than any teacher.

Advice for Busy Parents

If you claim that you haven't got time for your children, you're not alone. Others, too, have this problem and feel helpless to solve it. Busy parents are not necessarily irresponsible parents. They may simply be too busy with their jobs, community projects and benefiting the Jewish people or simply have large families and find it difficult to give each child the time and resources which he deserves.

Be partially consoled by the fact that, by age 8 or so, your child has probably *realized* you are busy, and that will make him treasure the time you *can* spare. Beyond that, try taking your child along with you to share a busy day. You'll be surprised at the opportunities for private time — even during such a day. What's more, your child will get a better picture of your day and feel closer to you, even when he's not there to share it. This point is so important that I want to make a potentially controversial statement: *Taking your child with you can be so beneficial to your relationship that it sometimes justifies taking him out of school for a day or a weekend.* Don't fret over missed schoolwork; your child will be more than happy to make it up. Hire a tutor if necessary. A parent-child "getaway" doesn't have to be done often, but do it.

Building Trust in Advance

Most relationships have their tough moments, especially when the interaction involved is frequent and intense. When you see someone often, and your relationship is highly emotional, difficulties are more likely to occur, both because of the amount of time you spend together and the emotional nature of the relationship.

Our ability to weather these "storms" generally depends upon our investment — quantitative and qualitative — in the relationship beforehand. When a relationship is solid, any inevitable misunderstandings or conflicts become less serious.

The most important element of this investment involves building trust. When I trust your motivations and your attitude toward me, I can more easily deal with any emotional "squalls" which may arise.

Trust is largely based upon honesty. Children particularly are hurt by even a minor breach of promise, often blowing it way out of proportion. Even a minor promise is major to a child.

I therefore strongly recommend striking the words "I promise" from your vocabulary when speaking with your children. Then, in an unusual situation, "I promise" can make a major impact, as is shown by the following poignant episode.

> Seven-year-old Chaya just had a spat with her twelve-year-old brother. As a parting shot, the boy taunted his sister by telling her she was adopted. The girl, believing her brother, ran to her room, buried her head in her pillow, and began to cry.
> Chaya's father entered his daughter's room and explained that, although being adopted was nothing to be ashamed of, he and her mother were in fact Chaya's biological parents. She continued to sob. Her father then asked, "Have I ever told you, 'I promise'?" His daughter shook her head. "Well," continued her father, "I promise that you aren't adopted." The girl immediately stopped crying, realizing that her older brother had merely taunted her.

Had this father used the words "I promise" in non-emergencies, this incident would not have been so quickly resolved. Build trust by saying, "I will try," and following through, but don't promise. The *Gemora*[6] itself warns against breaking promises made to children. In addition, to be totally honest with your children you must role-model this by never breaking a promise to them.

A promise is like a shout: Use it sparingly, if ever, in order that it be effective in the rare situation where it is appropriate.

Your Child is Your Most Important Guest

Another good piece of advice is to "schedule" your child in your datebook. After all, he is at least as important as your other appointments. Small chunks of time can be used to plan longer sessions, which of course can also be scheduled.

---

6. *Succah* 46b.

The following true story brings this idea into focus:

Well-known, busy Rav N. was once sitting and talking with his son Shmuel when an unexpected visitor arrived to see him. Rav N. replied, within earshot of his child, that he was busy. As he escorted his guest to the door, the rav quietly thanked his visitor for the opportunity to show Shmuel how important he was to his father.

Everyone agrees that guests deserve special consideration. Consequently, we are attentive, responsive, and accommodating toward them. Let us remember that our children are essentially our guests, for after twenty years or so, they'll be moving out. Although we certainly don't want to spoil them, and indeed many guests love to feel like "one of the family,"[7] and not be treated too royally, we want our children to enjoy their stay in our home — especially since, as someone once mentioned to me, we hope one day to be invited into *their* homes! So give your children your attention and make them feel welcome and wanted.

"Closed" Children

A major source of parental anguish is a "closed," uncommunicative child. Such withdrawal is unnatural. Have you ever seen an uncommunicative two-year-old? On the contrary, when something is on his mind, he lets you know. If you see a closed child, therefore, *something happened to him.* Prob-

---

7. Rashi on Bemidbar 29:36 says that a guest is served less sumptuous fare with each passing day. Others explain why: The mitzvah of hospitality involves making a guest feel at home. Only when he is finally served what the family eats does he feel completely at home.

ably no one listened to him. It's quite painful to try to communicate with someone and be ignored, and it's quite reasonable to eventually stop trying. It's human nature to try to avoid painful experiences.

This is not to say that you should begin a campaign to "open up" a retiring child. Never tamper too forcefully with a person's personality. It is almost irrelevant whether his quietness was caused by his environment, by his nature or by habit. Tred carefully, build trust, and eventually most people will once again tell you what's on their mind, just as they did when they were two years old.

So utilize your parental advantages. Set aside time for your children. Time and resources are the great advantages that a parent has over a teacher. Use these two advantages! A game, a story, or even a short trip together is a beautiful way to build — or strengthen — a positive relationship with your child. Be an example to him of what you'd like him to become. It's hard work, with instant results most definitely *not* guaranteed, but lay the foundation. Not only will you have less trouble later, but you'll also have a lot of *nachas*.

Foresight

Parents often neglect to forsee problematic situations. For instance, it's obviously better to "childproof" your house than to constantly shout at your three-year-old to stop wreaking havoc in a living room decorated with fancy and fragile objects. This fairly minor, temporary problem is a matter of short-term projection. Long-term problems, however, require greater foresight. Let's examine an important example of this.

Seeing Each Child as a Success

Some problems are years in the making, and are therefore highly difficult to solve. One such problem arises when parents fail to appreciate their children's traits and abilities. These differences need to be noticed and *appreciated* by parents.

Children differ in their character traits. They differ in their mental abilities and they can have a wide range of differences in aptitude. If, for example, a child is more capable than his older sibling in the areas which the parents most prize, trouble is brewing. Should the parents value scholastic achievement, and it's the younger child, for instance, who is more academically inclined, it will soon become obvious how much more *nachas* they have from the younger child. Even if they try to contain or subdue their happiness (which may be the wrong thing to do), the parents' deeper feelings will eventually be evident to all, especially to the older, less "successful" child. All sorts of problems are in the offing here, with disciplinary ones ranking high among them.

The older child may eventually reject his parents' values in favor of his own, according to which he is a "success," thereby causing conflict and hard feelings between himself and his parents. Alternatively, he will simply accept his parents' values, and feel second-rate, since he can't really compete with his younger sibling.

I'm not sure which result is worse. Either way, the parents should have forseen this problem and planned accordingly.

The Vilna Gaon[8] stresses that no two people are the

---

8. Mishlei 16:4. The *Gra* writes:

For each person has his own path to trod, for their minds are not the same, nor are their faces similar, and no two same. In fact, he writes, that the original and primary function of a prophet was to help each person find his own way of serving G-d. The *Sfas Emes*[9] tells us that each of the twelve tribes was represented by a differently colored stone in the high priest's breastplate, in order to emphasize the uniqueness of each tribe.[10]

Parents must internalize this lesson. Each child is a jewel in G-d's crown and parents are the polishers of these jewels. Learn to feel good about each of your children, just as Hashem Himself feels good about them.

In Summary

- Build a positive, trusting relationship with your child.
- Children want to love and respect their parents.
- Your child is your most important "guest."
- Learn to focus on your child's positive qualities.

---

men have the same nature. And when there were prophets, people would go to the prophets to 'seek out Hashem' (Bereishis 25:22), and the prophet, through prophecy, would tell them the path they should travel, each according to the root of his soul and his physical nature.

כי לכל אדם ואדם יש לו דרך בפני עצמו לילך בו, כי אין דעתם דומה זה לזה ואין פרצופיהם דומים זה לזה ואין טבע שני בני אדם שוה. וכשהיו נביאים היו הולכים אצל הנביאים לדרוש את ה׳ והיה הנביא אומר, על פי משפט הנבואה, דרכו אשר ילך בה לפי שורש נשמתו וטבע גופו.

9. Written by the Gerrer Rebbe, Rav Yehudah Aryeh Leib Alter (1847-1905), the *Sfas Emes* is an awe-inspiring work of immense scope and depth.
10. See the *Sfas Emes* on *parshas Noach*, p. 34, first column.

3

Two Enemies — Surprise and Laziness

Rav Tzodok HaKohen explains that the two major weapons of the *yetzer hora* (evil inclination) are *surprise* and *laziness*. These two problems also pertain to discipline.

Both surprise and laziness here refer to *thought*. We don't put enough thought into understanding our children, yet we are surprised and knocked off balance when unexpected things occur. We react immediately, without thinking, then fail to analyze what has just occurred.

---

1. As Rav Tzodok writes:

ועיקר תפיסת היצר הוא על ידי הזדמנות ויצרו משכיחו כרגע האיסור עד שהלב חומדו וכו' ועל ידי ריפוי ידים שהוא העדר הזריזות ועצלה תפיל תרדמה שהוא העדר הדעת והזכרון להתבונן.

"The major ploys of the evil inclination involve (1) a chance event in which the inclination causes you to momentarily forget a prohibition, whereby the heart lusts, etc. and (2) 'weakness of the hands,' which is a lack of zeal. Laziness brings about slumber, which is the lack of understanding and memory [needed] to think with understanding."

Resisei Lailoh, sec. 38

Thought is thus required — and too often missing — at three stages:
1. Understanding the situation before the problem arises.
2. Reacting to the problem.
3. Subsequently evaluating our reaction.

Perhaps the *Mesillas Yeshorim* (The Path of the Just)[2] alludes to this process in the beginning of chapter two:

הנה ענין הזהירות הוא שיהיה האדם נזהר במעשיו ובעניניו, כלומר מתבונן ומפקח על מעשיו ודרכיו, הטובים הם אם לא....

Watchfulness means that a man should exercise caution in his actions and affairs, to deliberate and watch over his actions and affairs, to evaluate whether or not they are good, lest he abandon his soul to the danger of destruction, G-d forbid, and follow his habits like a blind man in the dark.

Four key words must be translated carefully:
1. להתבונן
2. לפקח
3. מעשיו
4. דרכיו

With these four words, the *Mesillas Yeshorim* points out both *what* requires planning in life and *how* to plan for it.

Although the first word, להתבונן, is usually translated as "to deliberate," its grammatical structure reveals a deeper meaning. The word is reflexive, referring to an action you do to yourself. Therefore it literally means "to *give oneself* בינה, *understanding*." The word בינה is related to the word בונה, build. להתבונן, then, bespeaks a depth of understanding *within yourself* with which you can build, can create new axioms, and can learn to cope with a new situation or manage better with an old one.

Such deliberation should be undertaken *before* problems

---

2. Written by Rav Moshe Chaim Luzzatto, *zt"l* (1707-1746).

materialize, so that they will not catch you off guard when they do arise.

The second word, לפקח, means "to bring to light" or "to uncover."³ A פקח is someone smart enough to uncover the heart of a matter, whose senses are alert to any important stimulus. A "supervisor" is thus called a מפקח, since he must notice everything around him.

These two verbs, להתבונן and לפקח, signify the two stages of proper planning. The first stage is להתבונן, to examine the problem or situation at hand, to understand its basis, and to construct a strategy. The second stage is לפקח, to fine tune this strategy by evaluating the advisability of its every detail.

The third word used in the *Mesillas Yeshorim* is מעשיו, the actions⁴ employed in implementing one's plans. דרכיו, the fourth word, refers to the general pattern of one's life.⁵ מעשיו are analogous to one's footsteps, that is, his specific steps to reach his goals, while דרכיו refers to his general direction in life.

Thus the *Mesillas Yeshorim* seems to be discussing the aforementioned three phrases: before, during, and after a

---

3. We find the word מפקחין in *Yoma* 8:7, where the phrase "מפקחין עליו את הגל" denotes digging someone out from under a pile of rubble, literally "bringing him to light." *Tiferes Yisroel*, a commentary on the Mishnah, translates מפקחין here as "we open."

4. In a narrower sense, עשייה means "finalization," i.e., completing the final detail. As the Vilna Gaon explains in *Aderes Eliyahu* commenting on the beginning of *Sefer Bereishis*: עשייה can refer to the 'fixing,' i.e., the "finishing touches" of something's creation. Using this concept, the *Siddur HaGra* explains the phrase "עושה שלום" — literally, "the One Who makes peace" — as "the One Who perfects the world." Similarly, the *HaKesav VeHaKabbalah* on Bemidbar 15:22 tells us that עשייה refers to making something permanent.

5. As the Vilna Gaon comments on the verse "Do not go on the way" (Mishlei 1:15), דרך refers to the "broad, 'paved' road."

problem has presented itself.

The planning and projecting stage, during which potential problems are targeted and contingency plans made, is the להתבונן stage. Then comes לפקח, when the feasibility of the plan is examined in detail. Only afterwards does one take action, מעשיו, and work toward the long-term goals of דרכיו.

To quote *Mori VeRabi, zt"l*: When you plan and execute your child's *chinuch*, consider how your approach will affect him twenty years from now.

Successful discipline mandates identifying and remedying problems when our children are young — and applying the childrearing principles we've learned. This is the ideal time to pinpoint issues and then consult *rabbonim* and other authorities. *Personally, when a question involving my own children arises, and a more objective opinion is needed, I often consult others, but only after formulating the question myself.*

In summary, we must provide our children with the time and concentration they deserve. After all, they are our major "investment" in life. If we want them to mature into happy, successful people in the eyes of G-d and man, we must evaluate their needs as objectively as possible. Then we must take the time to consult others. Problems are part and parcel of childrearing in all its stages,[6] but, *b'ezras* Hashem, they need not take us by surprise, and we can have the strength to resolve them.

---

6. The Brisker Rov (Rav Yitzchok Ze'ev Soloveitchik (1889-1959), *zt"l*, is quoted as having said that childhood diseases are referred to as גידול בנים, raising children, for this is how children grow. (See *Chovos HaLevovos, Shaar HaBechina*, Ch. 5.) צער גידול בנים, on the other hand, the *pain* of raising children, refers to *chinuch*.

In Summary

- Our children are our most precious possessions. We must invest at least as much planning and interest in their *chinuch* as we would in any other of life's important projects.

4

Fair, Firm, and Friendly

*M**ori VeRabi, zt"l,* once stated that a good disciplinarian must be fair, firm, and friendly.

1. Fairness

Discipline must be fair and even-handed, both in your eyes and in your child's. If he perceives — even wrongly — that an injustice is being done, your disciplinary action will not succeed.

Therefore, a child should be involved in the disciplinary process. This involvement will increase as he grows in age and maturity. He is less likely to disobey rules that he himself has helped to establish.

In addition, in the name of fairness, give your child the opportunity to *explain* his misbehavior. Sometimes this can change your entire perspective on your child's "misbehavior" and the way you react to it, as the following true story demonstrates:

> *A teacher once received a phone call from a distraught mother who had just yelled at her child for drawing all*

over his cheeks with an orange marker.
The teacher asked the mother if she had inquired of her son why he had behaved this way. The mother replied that she had not. The teacher advised her to do so, after allowing for a brief wait to allow the air to cool.
When the mother later questioned her child, he explained that during supper she had mentioned to him that if he ate all of his vegetables, his cheeks would have a nicer color. He had simply tried to help things along.

If only this mother, rather than flying off the handle, had asked her child why he had done what he had done, things would have turned out differently.[1] Instead, the child felt, justifiably, that he had been treated unfairly. Such feelings undermine the spirit of future cooperation and trust which is vital to proper discipline.

2. Firmness

The limits which you impose on your child's activity must be firm. This does not mean that you can never be flexible, but your child must be clear about what he may and may not do. Such clarity makes for a calmer, more confident child and more effective discipline.

Children tend to test the outer limits of what is permitted, yet respect those boundaries if you are firm. Firmness means being calm and sure, *not* harsh or threatening.

Firmness also implies *consistency*. You must not give in

---

1. If it is clear, after the explanation, that there is a need to take disciplinary action, do not get involved in a debate. Once it is clear that the child has stated his view of the matter, firmly reiterate why it is wrong, and end the discussion.

to your child's insistent testing of your resolve. If you do, he is more likely to risk disobeying in the hope that he will get away with it. Certainly, then, you can't have a whole minefield of "don'ts," since your need to be firm under such circumstances would cause you to constantly confront your child for one misdemeanor or another, never giving in!

In addition, inconsistency conveys to your child that you yourself are not sure how important your rules are, and that's poor *chinuch*.

3. Friendliness

Despite the need to be firm, one must stay warm and caring.

If you aren't naturally warm or you find it difficult to transmit this feeling, don't attempt to change your personality. Instead, build on your strengths. Introduce your child to an activity you particularly enjoy, and do it together. People who enjoy the same things develop a certain camaraderie. In addition, *praise* your child whenever he deserves it.

Sometimes it is even a good idea to commiserate with your child when he protests some of your disciplinary guidelines. After all, you want your child to be your disciple.

Important Advice

Mori VeRabi, zt"l, advised a group of would-be *mechanchim* that when a child is undisciplined, it's *his* problem, not yours. With this approach you will then be more capable of being fair, firm, and friendly toward him. After all, since you are there to help him with *his* problem, you can remain objective and calm. When teachers or parents are overwhelmed by *their* problem, the stage is set for poor *chinuch*, and anger and harshness often replaces firmness.

In Summary

• Try and involve your child in establishing a behavioral code at home. This includes consequences for misbehavior.
• Be fair — allow your child to present his view of the situation before taking disciplinary action.
• Be firm — be consistent.
• Be friendly — remain warm and caring.
• **Remember — when a child lacks discipline it's *his* problem, you're just there to help him escape his behavioral rut.**

5

When Parents Disagree

Parents often disagree on how a child should be disciplined. Such differences of opinion are not necessarily bad, for two heads are often better than one. Indeed, "consultative disagreement" can not only yield better solutions, but it can also enhance a marriage, for working together on a problem can increase husband and wife's respect, caring and concern for one another.

HaGaon Rav Yitzchok Hutner, *zt"l*, writes very beautifully about this phenomenon.[1] The *Gemora* states that two scholars who "battle" each other end up loving each other.[2] Rav Hutner explains that precisely *because* they "battled" each other, disagreeing so vehemently, they came to love each other. Torah scholars essentially seek to understand what is truly G-d's will. Their "battling" with each other brought them closer to their goal, and their very opposition helped bring the truth to light.[3]

---

1. See *Pachad Yitzchok*, "*Chanukah*," end of *maamar* 3.
2. See *Kiddushin* 30b.
3. Likewise when parents disagree with each other and clarify what is

However, when parents don't see eye to eye on discipline, it is sometimes part of a broad pattern of disagreement between them. Such parents must *isolate* the discipline problem from their larger problems and deal with questions of discipline separately. They should not wait until the larger problems are solved. Any delay will only exacerbate the "smaller" problem of discipline, since misbehavior tends to worsen if it is not treated quickly. The older the child, the more ingrained his misconduct, and the greater will be the likelihood of additional disciplinary problems.

These parents should focus on the *reasons* for their disagreement on what constitutes good disciplinary practice. For instance, understanding how one's spouse was raised can shed much light on his or her approach to discipline. Such appreciation of each other's backgrounds can in turn illuminate a couple's broader problems as well.

Even healthy disagreement must be settled *before* disciplining your child. Conflicting disciplinary styles only encourage behavioral problems.

Having said this, however, it must be noted that mothers, by nature, commonly favor a softer approach, while fathers tend toward strictness.[4] These varying approaches, *if they do not stem from a larger pattern of marital discord*, are not

---

best for their child, not only will their child benefit, but they will enhance their own relationship as well.

See *Igros Moshe, Shulchan Oruch, Orach Chaim*, vol. IV, sec. 25, for a beautiful interpretation of the role of disagreement in understanding Torah.

Also see *Bava Metzia*, 84a, which describes how Rabi Yochanan was inconsolable over the death of Reish Lakish, his study partner, who had so "fought" with him over his Talmudic insights.

4. Rashi on Vayikra 19:3 states that a son fears his father more than his mother because she tends to speak gently.

necessarily counterproductive. This gender difference may be Hashem's way of applying the dictum that with a child you must "push away [i.e., be strict] with the left [hand] and draw close with the right."[5]

Mori VeRabi, zt"l, once depicted this idea very graphically. First he drew an object toward him with both hands. Then he pushed the object away, again with both hands. These two movements paralleled those of either two "right hands" or two "left hands;" in neither case was the object itself affected, just its distance from him. However, when his right hand drew the object closer and the left hand pushed it away, the object turned, i.e., it was *affected.* In the same way, we change and affect our children when we apply the dictum of the right hand drawing close and the left hand pushing away. Remember the right hand is the stronger one. You should affect your children more often with your warmth than through your "distance."

If, however, you openly disagree with your spouse on disciplinary measures your child will exploit this disunity by relying on his mother to save him from his father's wrath. His father may then tend to be more lenient than necessary, lest he always appear to be the "bad" parent in his child's eyes. Or, he may be more strict than he would like to be, in order to compensate for his wife's being "overly soft." Neither eventuality is to be desired.

Parents should therefore discuss past disciplinary problems and determine how to deal with them in the future. A mother *must not* say, "Wait until your father comes home!"[6] Instead she should make it clear that both parents have agreed to the consequences of the misbehavior. A father must em-

---

5. See *Sanhedrin* 107b and *Sotah* 47a.
6. It is forbidden to threaten a child with punishment without taking prompt action. See *Kitzur Shulchan Oruch*, 165:7.

phasize that his child's mother will not overturn his punishment. In other words, when the six-year-old hits his younger brother, the father should take his hand and say "Mother and I have decided that you must remain in your room if you hit someone. You may come out when you can behave pleasantly in other people's company."

In Summary

• Parental disagreement can be quite productive and beneficial to the child.

• Parents must put aside their general disagreements and focus on harmonizing their approach to solving their children's disciplinary problems.

• Parents can differ in their approach to discipline as long as:

1. This difference is not meant to undermine the position of the spouse vis-à-vis the children.

2. The parents agree on this difference in tactics *beforehand*, without arguing over it in their children's presence.

6

Honoring Parents — A חוק

Many of the Torah's mitzvos seem logical, but many do not. The Torah calls "*chukim*" statutes which have no obvious logic. *Mori VeRabi, zt"l,* notes that the word חוק connotes permanence, as in "חק נתן ולא יעבור"[1] ("He has given a statute that shall not pass away"). For this reason laws we consider logical are liable to change along with our own logic. *Chukim,* on the other hand, are beyond our understanding; we observe them purely out of servitude to Hashem.

As logical as the mitzvah of honoring and obeying parents is, it must *also* be taught as a חוק, for only then will it endure.[2]

Children often overlook what their parents do for them, and whatever gratitude one's children do feel tends to evaporate once he refuses their request. Therefore, children must be taught that honoring their parents is a *chok* — an immutable law applicable in all situations. As Rav Dessler, *zt"l,* writes, even well-behaved children must be *taught* to obey their

---
1. Tehillim 148:6.
2. See Rashi on Shemos 21:1. *All* the laws of the Torah, even the "logical" ones, are from Sinai and are hence immutable.

parents. This must not be left to their instincts.[3]

While your child should certainly learn to love and honor you out of gratitude, you cannot wait until he is mature enough to recognize everything you've done for him. Gratitude comes from the feeling of having received something which is not necessarily due as a matter of course. The younger the person, the more self-centered he is (as you well know, an infant is willing to wake up an entire continent just because he has a tickle in his throat!) and the more he feels that everything is coming to him. Consequently you must train your children, even at the tender age of two, to respect you.

Don't convey this message by hitting and shouting. *Calmly* remind them not to yell, ignore, or interrupt you. *Never* respond to a loud, shrill, or impatient retort or request. My wife tells the children, "When you scream, I can't hear you." When you address a young child and get no response, often it is because he is preoccupied, and not because he is being disrespectful. Children, especially young children, can become totally engrossed and fascinated by some new discovery. Approach the child, have him face you, and *calmly* repeat yourself. And avoid speaking more than a minute to two-year-olds; they have very short attention spans for things which do not interest them.

Even a two-year-old must treat you respectfully. When a child is that young, the mitzvah can be taught only as a *chok.* The main vehicle of this is *habituation.* Children must become accustomed to behaving respectfully toward their parents. Some even maintain that your child should address you

---

3. See *Michtav MeEliyahu,* vol. 3, pp. 360-62.
4. Others claim that such formality distances child and parent. Yet parents also have manifold opportunities to establish a wonderful relationship with their children. Thus parents should follow whatever is customary in their area. If neighbouring children address

in the third person ("*Abba* said" instead of "you said") and stand when you enter a room.[4] Such training is an ongoing reminder that parents must always be respected, no matter what. It's a *chok*.[5]

In Summary

• Children must be trained to obey their parents even before they can understand the rationale behind the mitzvah.

• Young children need to be *habituated* to respect and obey their parents.

• With a young child, do not interpret his lack of attention as a sign of disrespect. Young people are easily distracted. *Remain calm*, he probably does not mean to be insolent.

---

their parents by their *first names*, however, *move*, as this is indicative of a society where parents are certain to have trouble disciplining their children as they grow older.

5. In *Kad HaKemach*, כבוד אב ואם בהתחלת הערך, Rabbeinu Bachaya equates our responsibilities towards G-d and towards our parents, as both obligations are reflected in the first three of the Ten Commandments: (1) Just as we must acknowledge our Creator, we are required to acknowledge our earthly creators, our parents. (2) Just as we must not deny the existence of the Creator, we may not deny our parents' existence. (3) Just as we must not swear in G-d's Name falsely or in vain, we must not invoke the name of a parent falsely or in vain.

7

Making Yourself Understood — Before a Problem Arises

One main issue in any discussion of discipline involves proper communication, i.e., *clearly* telling our children the *kind* of behavior expected of them and the *consequences* of misbehavior. Disciplinary problems begin when children aren't sure about their parents' dos and don'ts or how firmly they will be enforced. Therefore, to impress upon your child how you expect him to behave, you must be both *clear* and *firm*.

Communication is not just what you say, it's how you say it. The tone, length, and timing of your remarks all convey your degree of firmness (or lack thereof). Non-verbal communication is another powerful tool. As the saying goes, silence speaks louder than words.

Clarity, however, depends upon well-chosen words. For example, you may urge your child to "Cross the street safely." "Safely" is too loose a term. Tell him instead, "Cross the street only at the corner. Even if the light is green, look both ways. If no cars are coming, put your right foot into the street. Then look both ways again. If there is still no traffic, put your left foot into the street. If there are still no cars coming, cross to the other side." Be verbal, specific, and clear.[1] Your child's obedience will improve simply because he will understand more of what you want of him.

When confronted with their disobedience, children often respond, "But I didn't understand." Your child is less likely to make such a claim when you are clear. Ask him to repeat your instructions — you'll often find that he has indeed misunderstood you or that he underestimated the importance of the issue. Alternatively, you may discover that you have forgotten important details.

As we noted above, your *tone* conveys a great deal. Words have a greater impact when they are spoken softly but firmly.[2] Timing is also important. If you give your directions as close as possible to their intended implementation, then they are more apt to be heeded.[3] To use our street-crossing example, if you give your child *specific* instructions *immediately before* he crosses the street, he will probably comply.[4]

---

1. The word לדבר refers to speaking in a commanding way. The עשרת הדברות (Ten Commandments) is a well-known example. Similarly, a spokesman who speaks with authority is called a דַבָּר. Likewise, Rabi Avohu, who represented his people in Rome, was called מדברנא דאומתיה, the one authorized to speak on behalf of his people (*Sanhedrin* 14a). In *Tzidkas HaTzaddik* (sec. 221), Rav Tzodok writes that the word לדבר connotes *specificity*. In addition, the *Shittah Mekubetzes* כתובות ז "בברכת איירוסין," maintains that the word "commanded" is used in the blessing "וצונו על העריות" recited under the *chuppah*, because the sexual prohibitions in the Torah are *explicitly* stated. Thus, a commandment should be both *specific* and *explicit*.
2. See Rav Shlomo Wolbe, *"Pelech HaShtikah U'Felech HaHodayah,"* secs. 1-3, where he argues that speech and silence are best when combined, i.e., by speaking briefly or softly.
3. See Rashi on Shemos 19:24.
4. In addition, if you speak softly but firmly, you stand a greater

Your child will usually bridle at behavioral limitations if he is already excited about things which he's doing or intending to do. However, if you express your disapproval *before* your child has his heart set on something, you stand a better chance of dissuading him without confrontation.[5] Such "friendly dissuasion" is eminently preferable, since confrontations rarely have winners. Should you "lose," you invite further challenges to your authority. And although your child has gotten his way, he, too, is a loser, since he knows he's won only by forcing the issue and causing you distress. This knowledge certainly doesn't help him think highly of himself. On the other hand, the amount of force you may need to "win" can result in too costly a "victory."

In summary, your child is more inclined to understand and accept your feelings if you present them before any problematic situation arises. Try to *project* situations and try to deal with them in advance. Before school vacation, for instance, establish with your child what constitutes acceptable and unacceptable vacation activities. Similarly, Thursday evening, anticipate when and where you will need help with Friday's Shabbos preparations.

In short, specific instructions should be given immediately before implementation, while broader behavioral patterns should be developed and clarified as far in advance as possible.

We don't always "brief" our children on how we'd like them to behave in various situations. We simply react on the spot, after a problem arises, but when we are less in control

---

chance of being obeyed. Naturally, early in your child's street-crossing career, you should be on hand to monitor his progress.

5. As is well-known, the best time to deal with temptation is before temptation arises. See *Divrei Yehoshua*, sec. 2, ch. 6; and *Chochmah U'Mussar*, vol. 1, *maamar* 229. Also see שיחות הרב חיים שמואלביץ, מאמר הרחקת האדם מן החטא.

and not in a position to clarify to them what kind of behavior we would have preferred. At such moments, we cannot deal with our children's emotions; it's quite enough just coping with our own.

It would be far better to pick a quiet time in pleasant surroundings to discuss these general or explicit and specific issues with our children ahead of time. For if we speak calmly and clearly, our children can be somewhat "programmed" to react as we see fit. Yet we must remain *open to their views* as well. Only then can we develop realistic expectations of our children. In addition, as mentioned earlier,[6] children are more likely to comply with a behavioral code which they themselves helped to formulate.

Avoid "Forecasting" Negative Behavior

Some parents inadvertently encourage misbehavior by "forecasting" it with remarks like "I'm warning you! Don't fight with your younger brother!" Other parents are less direct but nonetheless emphasize the punishment for breaking the rules, threatening "If you fight with your younger brother, I will spank you!" This emphasis conveys to your child that you *expect* him to misbehave.

Similarly, children frequently get "labeled": "You two just don't get along, do you? If this happens again, you'll both be severely punished." Once declared incompatible, children are likely to believe it.[7]

All such scenarios are dangerous, because children often

---

6. See p. 51.
7. See *HaBayis HaYehudi*, p. 449: "When you reprimand a child for some misbehavior, do not label him negatively, do not say to him, for example, 'You are a thief' or 'You are lazy,' etc."

do live up to our expectations, looking outside themselves for self-definition. A child learns right and wrong from parental reaction, so that activities which elicit punishment must be wrong, while those which prompt reward must be right. As he matures, his peers define right and wrong for him. Only when he reaches maturity do right and wrong become intrinsic values untempered by cultural whims. Avrohom Ovinu epitomized such maturity, since he defied the ideology of his entire generation.

When we *expect* our children to misbehave, they will more likely bear out our expectations. And threats of reprisal succeed only temporarily at best, for if your child continues to misbehave, as you've foretold, you'll have to regularly intensify his punishment.

On the other hand, if we are visibly confident — or at least hopeful — that our children can change, they probably will. Thus, when you say to your child, "I know you can handle the situation this time," you should also teach him how to do it. For if he fails again, his self-image will take a beating. After all, he will have let his parents down one more time.

Offering Solutions

The Vilna Gaon tells us that criticism should be coupled with constructive advice, thereby demonstrating a primary desire is to improve things, rather than merely finding fault.[8] Such advice, according to the Gaon, should both precede and follow any rebuke.

---

8. See the Vilna Gaon's commentary on Mishlei 24:26, in which he writes: "When you respond to [people] about improper things they have done, show them the proper path to follow."

"Advice" generally involves either clarifying a problem, which makes it easier to solve, or actually suggesting solutions. Let's take a common household conflict as an example — a child who is constantly "bothering" an older sibling.

You can offer specific solutions, such as, "When your younger brother angers you, either distract him with a toy or call me." Should the younger child be too old to be distracted, you can show the older one how to include him in his sibling's activity, thus making him feel part of things, rather than a nuisance.

Another approach can help clarify the problem. First, offer validity to your older child's frustration by saying, "It must really be tough having your younger brother always on your back." Such commiseration makes him feel that you understand him and it is a good way to gain his cooperation. He will help solve the problem because he isn't being branded "the bad one." You can then say how the house sometimes gets pretty crowded and discuss what can be done about it; or suggest to your older child how important he must be to the younger one. These non-judgmental approaches may change the older child's perspective and make it easier to solve the problem. For instance, if the older child spends some time with the younger one, the latter might more willingly allow the former some privacy in the future.

In this chapter, we have set forth some guidelines for *preventing* misbehavior by means of clear communication and proper expectations. In the next chapter, we will discuss how to *react* to misbehavior once it has already occurred.

In Summary

- Be clear and specific.
- Repeat your instructions as close to their proposed implementation as possible.
- Forbid activity which you don't want before your child has his heart set on it.
- Try to project possible problematic situations and discuss them with your child before they occur.
- Ask your child to repeat your instructions back to you.
- Don't predict misbehavior.

8

Making Yourself Understood — Afterwards

Rebuke — A Vital Skill

Effective rebuke is indispensable in communicating with children, as well as in all other relationships. In this chapter, we'll define constructive criticism, and then discuss how it applies to discipline. Just as many disciplinary problems can be avoided by the parents' clear, unambiguous expression of their expectations *before* difficulties arise, parents also need to know how to express their disapproval *after* the fact.

The Hebrew word for "reproof," תוכחה, derives from the word להוכיח (to demonstrate),[1] for as Rashi comments, תוכחה means clarification.[2] Thus, telling someone off — whether he is an adult or a child — isn't תוכחה. If you haven't shown your child, in a way he can readily understand, *why* you are displeased with his behavior, then you haven't reproved him in the Torah sense of the word. Consequently, don't expect his

---

1. Similarly, the Hebrew word for debate is ויכוח, because true debate is not merely an exhibition of sophistry or wit, but a honing of ideas in pursuit of the truth.
2. See Rashi on Bereishis 20:17, "ולשון תוכחה בכל מקום ברור דברים."

misconduct to stop or even to decrease. This is because giving someone a piece of your mind only damages your relationship with him, making it harder for him to see your side of things in the future.

True, telling off a child may temporarily frighten him into submission, but his fear will diminish as he matures. Never having been shown the error of his ways, he'll eventually ignore your strictures.

It is therefore vital that we learn to give תוכחה properly. Fortunately, our Torah provides us with beautiful, detailed advice on how to conduct ourselves before, during, and after the moment of reproach.

Let us first examine the period *before* any reproof is administered.

Patience

The *Gemora* tells us that reprimanding others requires infinite patience, for one may have to repeat himself as many as one hundred times.[3] Admittedly, the person being reprimanded can become jaded by seemingly endless sermonizing, but all of us — especially children — must be reminded of our obligations. Whoever is doing the reminding should stay calm and, if possible, should try to find different ways of saying the same thing so as not to sound like a nag.

The importance of remaining patient and hopeful cannot be overestimated. As the *Zohar* tells us, as long as a parent believes that his child can improve, this "awakening from below" (to use the Kabbalistic term) inspires a corresponding "awakening from Above," i.e., a positive Divine intervention.[4]

"But how can I stay patient?" you may ask. We all know

---

3. See *Bava Metzia* 31a: "אמר ליה, יוכיח תוכיחו אפילו מאה פעמים".
4. See *Zohar*, Vayikra 31b.

how difficult that can be, especially with loved ones. Their misdeeds upset you, not only because you see how such actions can harm them, but because parents tend to blame themselves for many of their children's faults. While studying the following advice on how to develop your power of patience, remember: The Vilna Gaon writes that the reiteration of your reproof is a sign of love.[5]

Notice Even Slight Improvements

Start noticing even the slightest improvements in behavior. It will give both you and your child hope, making it easier to be forbearing and remain calm.

Improvement can be measured in several ways:

1. *Frequency*: A reduction in the *frequency* of a *specific* form of misbehavior is one of the best signs that there has been movement in the right direction. Don't expect things to change overnight, but if even one type of negative behavior is happening less frequently, take heart.

2. *Intensity*: If your child's outbursts become less emotional, it's a good sign. Allow yourself to feel encouraged! For

---

5. See the Vilna Gaon's commentary on Mishlei 3:12, in which he notes that, unlike a friend, not only will a father reiterate his reproof, but he will explore any means of helping his child mend his ways, however painful this process may initially be. Yet corporal punishment can be used only with the greatest caution and after ample consultation. Many of today's Torah leaders feel that our generation is not "built" for such punishment.
In addition, when you have decided to use corporal punishment, it should not be harsh. A slap on the backside should be symbolic of the degree of your dissatisfaction. When used infrequently, it will have the desired effect.

example, fits of temper may still occur, but if there is any reduction in the intensity of the anger, then it is cause for hope.[6]

3. *Behavioral Threshold:* Improvement can also be measured by the degree of provocation required to trigger the misbehavior. To again use the example of a bad temper: In the past, a minor incident would have been sufficient to trigger a major outburst of anger, it now seems that something more provocative has to occur before the person loses control of himself.

Noticing these strides can calm you down, thereby enabling you to find appropriate words of encouragement for your child. Indeed, you should accustom yourself to congratulating your child on his improvement. Remember: Children

---

6. Frequency and intensity are mentioned in several important works: Rav Tzodok HaKohen writes: "Everyone should know that wherever his [evil] inclination attacks him most fiercely [a reference to intensity] is the area in which he has the potential to be particularly pure. The areas in which he has sinned particularly often [a reference to frequency] are the same areas in which he can be clean and pure hearted" (*Tzidkas HaTzaddik,* sec. 49). Similarly, in sec. 181 Rav Tzodok points out that where a person's evil inclination is most fierce, therein lay the person's greatest potential for perfection. He states, "Every person has his own particular lust, and in that area where his desire and lust are most overwhelming [a reference to intensity], in this very thing he has the potential to receive Hashem's blessing" (ibid., sec. 181).

The *Toras Avrahom,* written by the last *mashgiach* of Slabodka Yeshiva, may Hashem avenge his blood, Rav Avrohom Grodzinski, makes the same point: "And [one should] clearly distinguish between minor and major faults and between those that are both less bothersome and sporadic [frequency] and those that are more bothersome [intensity] and constant [frequency]" (p. 392).

generally don't *want* to misbehave or frustrate their parents. Telling them how pleased you are with their progress gives them an incentive to continue.

However, don't make your child feel that no matter how much he improves, you'll always expect more. Even if there's more "work" to be done, sometimes you must keep it to yourself and express your complete satisfaction with him, just the way he is!

To this end, you must realize that your child is not you. That is, your lively, boisterous son or daughter might never acquire your own quieter temperament. *This is a vital point.* Your patience must be attuned to realistic expectations of your child.

In summary, don't speak to your child until you are able to control of your emotions. Be patient. Notice your child's progress. And be calm and encouraging, even amid rebuke.

Let us now focus on two final important factors in successful reproof, which must be addressed before you even utter one word.

Your Relationship with Your Child

Rabbeinu Yonah[7] tells us that one primary function of a friend is to reprimand.[8] This idea carries with it the implication that effective reproof must come from a friend.

---

7. One of the great *rishonim*, Rabbeinu Yonah (1200-1263) authored the famed *Shaarei Teshuvah* (Gates of Repentance).
8. See Rabbeinu Yonah's commentary on *Pirkei Avos* 1:6, in which he writes: "...the second [function of a friend] is for mitzvos.... Sometimes he will misbehave [and] benefit from his sin, but it is neither his desire nor his will that his friend should commit it [this sin]...as a result, both will repent." Thus, because of his objectivity, a friend will see to it that his friend lives properly.

Thus, as we've mentioned elsewhere, a good relationship with your children is vital in order to speak with them effectively and without aggravation. This doesn't mean that your child should regard you as a peer. Rather, he should know that you understand him and that he has reason to trust that your advice will be to his benefit.

Timing

Choose the right moment to express displeasure. When your child — or anyone else, for that matter — is discouraged or anxious, that's not the time to tell him how unhappy you are with his behavior. He feels bad enough as it is.

Good timing makes your words far more likely to be accepted. As Rashi points out, Moshe waited until shortly before his death to rebuke his people.[9] We tend to cherish what we are about to lose, and everyone knew Moshe would soon die. It was an opportune moment to deliver an important message.

Having discussed what to bear in mind before starting to talk, we may now proceed to some guidelines for the actual delivery of your reproof.

Don't Label

Avoid labeling your child. If he has stolen, do not tell him, "You are a thief!" Rather, say, "You have stolen."[10] If we

---

9. See Rashi on Devorim 1:3. "This teaches us that he did not rebuke them until he was near death. From whom did he draw this lesson? From Yaakov, who did not rebuke his children until close to his death."
10. See ch. 7, footnote 7.

tell our children they are bad, they will believe us. A youth instinctively perceives himself as others perceive him, for his internal world is still incomplete and fluid. Young children in particular often see themselves as their parents and teachers do (whereas teenagers commonly rely on peer evaluation). So identify the misdeed without labeling the perpetrator.

Positive Labeling

Positive labeling, on the other hand, is highly recommended. The *Chovos HaTalmidim* instructs us to tell our children: "For someone as wise as you, such poor behavior is simply unfitting."[11] Label your child "wise," "mature," "understanding," etc., and he will try to live up to your estimation. Of course, positive labeling succeeds only if you believe what you're telling your child. Your sincerity makes all the difference.

---

11. See the introduction to *Chovos HaTalmidim*, entitled " שיח עם המלמדים ואבות הבנים ." There the author writes: "The *Shelah* (1560-1630) lights our way regarding the education of our generation in his comment on the verse 'Do not reprove the mocker, lest he hate you, reprove the wise man and he will love you.' (Mishlei 9:8) 'When you are about to reprove someone, do not denigrate him by calling him a mocker, for then he will hate you and not heed you. Rather, 'reprove the wise man,' saying to him, 'aren't you wise? Why should you behave this way?' Then 'he will love you' and heed you."

Offer Advice

According to the Vilna Gaon, reprimands should be accompanied by constructive advice.[12] Such suggestions imply that you consider your child sensible enough to profit from your rebuke and improve himself.

Another important point to bear in mind while you're talking to your child is the need to protect his dignity as much as possible. This is one of the reasons for our next suggestion.

Be Indirect

None of us like to be proven wrong. Even the best of us have trouble admitting our mistakes.

The *Shach*[13] tells us that whenever someone takes a position, he defends it; "דעביד איניש לאחזוקי דיבוריה," "A man is prone to uphold his words," sometimes even to the point of perjury.[14] How much more is a person prone to uphold his words past the point of objective reasoning. It becomes a personal matter: This is *his* opinion and he must show that his stance is correct.

Our egos can manifest themselves positively or negatively. Positively speaking, this can spur us to accomplish great things and behave with dignity, thereby living up to our

---

12. See the Vilna Gaon's commentary on Mishlei 1:25, in which he writes: "A loving person first advises that [his friend] should travel the proper path, and when [this friend] does not heed him and travels on the improper path, then he rebukes him for traveling the improper path."
13. Known acrostically as the *Shach*, Rav Shabse HaKohen (1622-1663) wrote one of the greatest commentaries on the *Shulchan Oruch* (Code of Jewish Law).
14. See the *Shach* on *Shulchan Oruch, Choshen Mishpat* 32:9.

own self-esteem. *But this pride also makes it hard, when confronted directly, to concede that we are wrong.*

It is therefore better to rebuke *indirectly*. For example, make your point at the Shabbos table in the form of a story or an appropriate saying of the Sages. Of course, this must be done in a manner whereby none of the other siblings understand whom you are reprimanding. Such subtle reproach prevents your child from becoming defensive, for he doesn't feel that he's under attack.

If you want to address your child directly, however, *defend him before you even begin*, saying something like "You were probably very upset by your younger brother. He constantly seems to be looking over your shoulder and disturbing you." This way, you show your child that you are trying to understand his position and that he hasn't lost any of your esteem.

Remember: People defend their positions to the very end, so don't force your child to defend himself.

Be Honest

Don't be devious with your child. By indirect rebuke, we do *not* (as a rule) mean that you pose a "hypothetical" case to your child and ask his opinion, then expose him as the real culprit in your "what if" scenario. Even if you stop short of the "punch line" ("Ahaa, that's exactly what *you* did!"), such an approach almost always loses more than it gains. A point may well be made, but the next time you pose a similar question, your child will be wary of being "set up" again.

If Possible, Not in Public

Like everyone else, healthy children have healthy egos. They are far less likely to admit to wrongdoing if others, especially siblings, are present. The *Gemora* tells us that Yerovam ben Nevot, the first king of the Ten Tribes, merited royalty because he had the courage to reprimand Shlomo HaMelech, but lost his share in the World to Come because he did so in public.[15]

Even when a child *should* be rebuked in the presence of his siblings — for example, if he has openly flouted your authority — proceed with caution. One of the first and foremost guidelines to remember is to warn your children *in private* that if they try to undermine your parental position, you will have to respond publicly.

Speak Calmly

Respond to attacks on your authority *calmly*, because an emotional reaction will communicate to your children that you really *do feel* threatened to some extent.

As in all communications with your children, speak softly but firmly. In addition, be as brief as possible, but not too brief. Make sure you are understood, then rest your case.

We can now look at the final phase of successful reproof, the period *following* the actual reprimand.

---

15. See *Sanhedrin* 101b.

Follow Up with Soft Words

According to the Vilna Gaon when a person loves someone, he concludes his reproof with soothing words.[16] Yet this comfort should not be extended immediately, or the child might think you are retracting your rebuke, a misunderstanding that will undermine any future reproof.

As the *Mishna* tells us, don't try to console someone while he is upset.[17] Wait ten or fifteen minutes. (This interval varies, of course, with the circumstances and the child's temperament.)

This idea may be part of what the *Gemora* means by "pushing away" a child with your left hand (i.e., keeping a certain distance and stature vis-à-vis your child, thereby instilling within him an appropriate degree of awe) and "drawing close" with your right (i.e., developing a warm relationship).[18] That is, that *after* you have put some "distance" between you and your child in the form of rebuke, bring him close again.

Remember, the right hand is the stronger one. You should affect your children more often with your warmth than through your "distance."

Incidentally, by envisioning the right hand — a symbol of strength — as the hand that "draws close," this *Gemora* seems to stress closeness over distance. So remember, put at least as much effort into building a warm and productive relationship with your child as you would invest in disciplining him.

No doubt about it: Effective rebuke doesn't always come easily. On the other hand, there is probably no better way to imbue your children with your values.

---

16. See the Vilna Gaon's commentary on Mishlei 3:12. See footnote no. 5.
17. See *Pirkei Avos* 4:19.
18. See *Sanhedrin* 107b and *Sotah* 47a.

In Summary

- Notice and react positively to even slight improvements.
- Choose the right time to offer reproof.
- *Don't give your child a negative label.*
- Offer advice.
- Be indirect.
- Be honest.
- Don't rebuke in public.
- Speak calmly.
- Follow up with soft words.

9

Time It Right

As we have discussed in chapter 8, timing is an important element of discipline. The Mishnah tells us, "Do not appease your friend in his moment of anger; do not comfort him while his deceased lies before him; do not question him while he is making a vow..." (*Pirkei Avos* 4:19).

According to the Maharal the common denominator in all of this Mishnah's examples is that all these actions lead us *away* from our goal. The Maharal gives us a golden rule: "...For whenever someone is intense in a given area, if his friend tries to oppose him and negate this intensity, he will react with even greater intensity."[1]

---

1. See *Derech Chaim*, the Maharal's commentary on *Pirkei Avos*:

כי כל מי שמתגבר בדבר אחד, אם בא חבירו כנגדו לבטלו מזה הוא מוסיף עוד יותר כנגד המבטל.

"Because when anyone is caught in an overwhelming situation (whether he is being overwhelmed or he is seeking to overwhelm with force a given situation), if (at that point) his friend will try to force him to refrain, then this will cause an even more forceful reaction."

When a person is stumbling, disappointed, or incapacitated, that's not the time to "put him in his place." Nor is it even the time to offer comfort. For as the Maharal points out, the same words that could have been so effective later will make the person even angrier if the person has already heard them when he wasn't yet capable of accepting them. For the worse he feels, the less likely he is to accept rebuke or encouragement.[2]

All the more so, then, that a child who feels depressed will tend to resent discipline. Even if he obeys, he does so out of hopelessness or disrespect for himself. Such "obedience" does not last, and eventually it can even turn the child against his parents. After all, when he was down and out, instead of empathizing with him, his parents "disciplined" him.

So before exercising your authority, take a long look at your child — his face, his situation, his frustrations. Reconsider. Is it the right time to discipline him? The following example is a case in point:

> *Yankel arrives home from cheder after doing poorly on an exam. Seeing his disappointment, his mother chooses not to mention that he did not make his bed that morning, nor does she sermonize about developing better study habits. Any "consequences" she may have planned are shelved. Instead, she empathizes with him over his poor performance at school. Only after a hearty supper and a good night's sleep does she bring up his room or his study habits.*

The timing has to be right not just for your child but for you, too. If you are too busy giving the children supper, or

---

2. This is one reason why the obligation to verbally comfort a mourner begins only after the mourner himself starts to speak. See *Shulchan Oruch, Yoreh Deah* 376:1.

preparing a class and cannot devote yourself to the problem at hand, then this is no time for discipline.

This point cannot be overemphasized. You must not determine your reactions to misbehavior in advance, and then blindly follow through with them. Any punitive situation is fluid. Your child may become contrite, he may offer a reasonable alternative to the penalty you had in mind, or, on the other hand, he may prove ruder or more obstinate than expected, thus necessitating stricter punishment. If you cannot focus on the situation at hand, or if you are in a rush, then defer dealing with it. Do not use "hit and run" tactics with your child.

Furthermore, while children *can* often resent being punished, children *certainly* resent not being given proper attention. If you punish them offhandedly, you are adding insult to injury, and your disciplinary action will almost certainly be fruitless.

If misbehavior cannot be dealt with when it occurs, you have two options:

You can wait until it happens again and then remind your child of his repeated offenses whereupon he will understand the need for appropriate action.

Preferably, however, wait until things are calmer and then discuss the matter with your child. Do not wait too long, though, lest he think that you harbor complaints against him. Besides making you a poor role model, such ambiguity can leave your child confused and insecure about where he stands with you.

In Summary

- Make sure the time is appropriate for disciplinary action, both for your child and for you.

10

Responding Right

The Hebrew word for "honor," כבוד, derives from כָּבֵד, heavy, for to honor something means to give it weight. Even in English, "weighing" a question implies comparing the importance of each factor. As one of our Torah leaders[1] once said, wisdom is the ability to differentiate not between what's important and what isn't but between what's important and what's *more* important.[2]

A parent must help his child develop this ability. One way children learn is by watching their parents "weigh" situations. If you react more sharply to a spill on the carpet than to your child's dishonesty, you are teaching him that ruining the carpet is worse than lying. Likewise, the more positive

---

1. HaGaon HaRav Abba Berman, *shlita*, *rosh yeshiva* of Iyun HaTalmud, Yerushalayim.
2. See HaGaon HaRav Yeruchem Levovitz, *zt"l*, *Daas Chochmah U'Mussar*: "For the foundation of foundations, the essence of man, is to recognize value and importance." Man can be great only if he can give honor where it is due. Rav Yeruchem devotes several chapters, replete with Torah sources, to this idea.

your response to his good deeds, the more he will want to repeat them.

In Hebrew, a young person is called a נער, a word whose root means "shake out" or "empty out." This is because young people are empty vessels just waiting to be filled with information and insight. Have you ever seen an infant who was not curious? Admittedly, some adults are no longer interested in learning, but this means that they have lost some of their humanity, for man is a learning machine.³ Children, then, are learning machines *par excellence*, well aware that they have an infinite amount to learn. Thus, the prophet states: "When Yisroel was a youth [נער], I loved him..." (Hoshea 11:1).⁴

Similarly, the Midrash⁵ explains that the words "and [Yosef] was a נער" (Bereishis 37:2) allude to Yosef's gift of prophecy.⁶ In a sense, a prophet empties himself in order to contain the Word of Hashem. (Although נער also means "fool" in Yiddish, this is probably because a fool, too, is empty but does not know it.)

---

3. See *Maharal, Nesivos Olom, Nesiv HaTorah*, Ch. 9, in which he writes that even in the World to Come, Hashem rewards the righteous with the opportunity to continue learning.
4. See *Chochmah U'Mussar*, vol. I, sec. 190, p. 344, where the *"Alter,"* *zt"l*, quotes Socrates as saying that all his wisdom lay in the fact that he knew that he didn't know. The author adds in the name of Rav Yisroel Salanter, *zt"l*, that the value of youth lies in a young person's realization that he has a lot to learn. Hence the cherubs which adorned the Ark containing the Tablets of the Law, for whoever has their youthful flexibility is beloved to Hashem.
   Interestingly, in *Machshevos Charutz*, sec. 7, p. 33 (יו) Rav Tzodok HaKohen notes that the word "philosopher" is Greek for "lover of wisdom."
5. See *Tanchuma Yoshon*, brought in *Torah Sheleima* Bereishis 37, sec. 32.
6. See Rav E. E. Dessler, *Michtov MeEliyahu*, vol. 3, pp. 127-28.

Children are always picking up on things, and your reactions inform them of your ideas about various issues. *They are likely to incorporate these ideas into their own world view.*

Your child's evaluation of your feelings about life will affect your ability to discipline him. Only when you demonstrate that certain values and activities are important to you, will he believe that you will insist upon them.

Make sure, too, that your reaction reflects the relative importance or unimportance of the situation. Fatigue, stress, and other factors can cause you to overreact. As difficult as it may be, don't let temporary circumstances affect your response.

This challenge involves two phases:

1. Before Things Get Tough

When your children come home from school, they are apt to be hungry. They may be tense because of something which happened that day. They deserve your full and calm attention. So, fifteen minutes before their arrival, refresh yourself with a nutritious snack, and consider the importance of welcoming them home with a smile, especially if they've had a rough day. They are likely to mirror your mood and think fondly of home as a nice place to come to. Most wives understand the value of greeting tired husbands properly, putting their own legitimate grievances aside while their spouses recharge. Children need the same treatment.

Of all one's childhood memories, what one remembers perhaps most is how it felt to come home. If your child thinks of home as a nice place to be, he won't stay away in later years, when children tend to go off with their friends. Instead, he'll bring his friends with him. Having your home serve as your children's meeting place has many and varied benefits, which are beyond the scope of this work. Suffice it to say that it's worth getting into the habit of thinking about these things before your child bursts through the door.

> *One mother of six lively boys bakes cookies a short time before the gang comes home from school, and then lies down to rest. She gets up just before they return. The resulting combination of a delicious aroma and her smiling face tells her children, "I'm happy you're home."*

2. When He's Home Already

Once your child has returned home and eaten something, ask him how his day went and *listen to his response.* If he learns from experience that his thoughts genuinely interest you, then if something has gone wrong that day, you'll hear about it. Once you know something is troubling him, you'll be better equipped to deal with his behavior. If your children all come home at the same time, then checking in with them all will take some planning, but make a habit of it. For if your child knows he will be heard every afternoon, he'll be more likely to wait his turn.

In summary, the younger the child, the more he learns from your reactions, both positive and negative. So make sure that your reactions are benevolent and just.

In Summary

- Make sure that your response to your child's misbehavior is in keeping with the degree to which you feel such behavior is inappropriate.
- Do not let external circumstances or your own fatigue cause you to overreact to behavior whch doesn't merit too strong a reaction. Save strong words for serious matters.

11

Who Are *You*?

Much has been written about role models in childrearing. Although our discussion is confined to discipline, it will be helpful to define role models and to explain why they are vital to all facets of successful childrearing, including discipline.

Seeing is Believing

We are deeply impressed by what we see, because images convey ideas forcefully and emotionally. The saying "seeing is believing" has more than a grain of truth to it. Indeed, Rashi tells us that certain sights solidify our faith,[1] and *Sefer HaKuzari* encourages us to *picture* the milestones of Jewish history.[2] What we see has an enormous impact on us.[3]

---

1. See Rashi on Shemos 20:19, where he writes: "There is a difference between what one sees and what others describe to him, for [regarding the latter], sometimes he's unsure as to whether to believe [it]."
2. See *Sefer HaKuzari*, part 3, no. 5.
3. Suffice it to say that the greatness of previous generations lay largely

Suffice it to say that what we see is essential to perfecting our inner world. "Role modeling" means *demonstrating* the ideas we wish to inculcate in our children by harnessing this all important sense of sight.

Our Own Torah

Another equally important advantage of role modeling is that it involves no direct teaching; rather, the child observes and *draws his own conclusions.* This type of learning is as meaningful to your child as it was to our Sages: As the *Gemora* tells us, whatever a Sage derived through his own efforts was especially beloved to him.[4]

This love for one's own conclusions is an expression of

---

in what they *saw.* Although ideas can be transmitted from generation to generation, experiences cannot. For example, even as the theory of evolution took the world by storm, Rav Naftoli Amsterdam, *zt"l,* (1832-1916) was unfazed, not because he could refute Darwinism intellectually but simply because, as he said, "I knew Rav Yisroel Salanter (1810-83). Rav Yisroel Salanter was *not* descended from an ape!" (Rav Shlomo Wolbe, *shlita, Alei Shor,* vol. 1, p. 57). As the *Gemora (Brochos* 20a) states, the later generations may have studied more, but their predecessors were more willing to sacrifice for Torah, *an emotional quotient.* Similarly, in the *Siddur Iyun HaTefillah,* p. 99, Rav Yaakov Tzvi Mecklenberg, *zt"l* (a giant of eighteenth-century German Jewry and a student of the legendary Rabbi Akiva Eiger, *zt"l),* quotes the great Yaavetz, *zt"l* (1435-1507), who lived through the Spanish expulsion, and had this to say: Those whose Judaism was "intellectual" couldn't bear to leave Spain and all their possessions, so they became Marranos. The women and simple folk, on the other hand, endured the tribulations of exile, for their faith was emotional.

4. See *Bava Kamma,* 17b.

the fact that man instinctively loves himself.[5] This love extends to his possessions[6] and, as we have just seen, to his ideas. As *Mori VeRabi, zt"l*, noted, "man dwells on *his* Torah day and night."[7] What we perceive as our own Torah has particular meaning for us.

The importance of role modeling may be demonstrated by a scene I witnessed many years ago:

> *A father once complained about his son to Rav Hershel Zaks, zt"l, then the principal of an elementary school in Yerushalayim. He has such a temper!" the father exclaimed. Rav Hershel listened patiently and then asked him, "Sir, do you have a temper?"*

Our children observe us to an unbelievable extent, and they can sense our feelings and values. As Rav Tzodok HaKohen puts it, a child's actions express what is hidden in the deepest recesses of his parent's soul.[8] And as the Chazon Ish, *zt"l*, wrote, students learn more from their teachers' actions than from their words.[9] This rule holds true for the child-parent relationship as well.

---

5. The Torah tells us that we must "love our fellow man as ourself" (Vayikra 19:18), implying that it is assumed we will love ourselves.
6. See *Siddur HaGra*, where the Vilna Gaon maintains that the word חוס in "*Shema Koleinu*" refers to one's special regard for his property.
7. Tehillim 1:2.
8. See *Tzidkas HaTzaddik*, sec. 63.
   Today, however, when our children begin school at such a tender age and are inundated with so many alien values, this rule — although still quite important — is not a reliable indicator of parental aspirations and values.
9. See the Chazon Ish, *Emunah U'Vitochon*, ch. 4, sec. 16: שלומד ממעשיו יותר משיעוריו .

Role-Modeling Discipline

S*elf-discipline* is even more difficult to teach than parental discipline. Most children, Rav Hirsch, *zt"l*, says, do not see self-discipline in their parents. Parents issue commands but don't seem to obey any themselves. *This is possibly why it is so difficult to teach children self-discipline.* In a Torah-true home, however, children see their parents subjugating themselves to their Creator. This subordination serves as an inspiring example to their children.[10]

In addition to Torah observance, many parents role-model discipline and respect in their relationship with *their* parents. When children see their grandparents treated with deference and respect, the lesson is not lost on them. Should grandparents be of a sometimes difficult nature, then their child-parent should regard this as a gift from Heaven. As your children mature, they will marvel at how well you manage to honor your parents even under the most difficult circumstances, and they will follow suit. The lesson will not be lost on them and it will translate into rich dividends in their future behavior towards you, especially if you won't be so cantankerous. This realization will help carry you through some stormy periods.

I cannot conclude without stressing the importance of how we treat our spouses. If parents respect each other, their children will too. So try to settle differences of opinion privately and amicably. The resulting atmosphere in the home will provide manifold benefits, including a family tendency to consider each other's wishes.

---

10. See Rav Shamshon Raphael Hirsch, *Yesodos HaChinuch*, part 2, p. 56.

In Summary

- Children learn best by modeling their parents' behavior. What they see is what you get!

12

Always Finding Fault?

Our self-image is intertwined with how others view us. Only the greatest people are impervious to disapproval and disagreement, remaining steadfast in their beliefs and way of life regardless of other people's opinions. Avrohom Ovinu was such a person. That's why he was called "העברי" (the one who stood on the side), for he retained his principles even when the entire world stood "on the other side."[1] (In truth, however, even Avrohom Ovinu's resolve was based on his knowledge that he had the *Ribono Shel Olom*'s approval and therefore was *not* standing alone.)

The Rambam stresses our vulnerability to environmental influence, for we gradually adopt local practices.[2] Furthermore, as Jews, the greater our exposure to an alien culture, the less sure we become of our "normalcy" in the face of a

---

1. See *Bereishis Rabbah* 42:8.
2. See Rambam, *Mishneh Torah, Hilchos Dei'os* 6:1, in which he writes: "Man by nature is drawn, both in his attitudes and in his actions, after his friends and behaves in accordance with the behavior of the people of his country."

host environment that considers us "off."[3] Such societal pressure weakens even the "strongest" among us, as the following true story illustrates:

> In America of the 1950s, beards were highly unusual, even for rabbis. Thus, when a prominent rav once visited a congregant in a mental hospital, the patients began to laugh and guffaw at the sight of his bearded face. Despite his strength of character and his pride in his ideals, this rav later admitted that he had felt momentarily ashamed.

If even such a fiercely independent *rav* could be embarrassed by the jeers of the mentally ill, how much more is the average adult's self-image affected by the perceptions of the "normal" people around him. *And if adults are this vulnerable, how much more so are children.*

Mori VeRabi, zt"l, likened children to new immigrants, for both observe the "inhabitants'" behavior and adjust their own conduct — and their self-image — accordingly. A child's sense of self-image is even more affected by how *his parents* perceive him. And what they *actually* think of him is perhaps less crucial than what he *imagines* they think.

A person's behavior generally reflects his self-image. One who sees himself, for example, as low, irresponsible, and selfish usually behaves in kind, whereas one who has been led to believe that he's noble and distinguished will also act

---

3. See Rav Avigdor Miller, *shlita, Praise, My Soul* (Brooklyn, 1982), p. 417, where the author explains that when we beseech Hashem to humble the wicked ("מכניע זדים") we are asking that no respect be accorded them; "for the respect to the wicked is a great harm to the cause of righteousness. The truth is enhanced by the scorn of falsehood: [hence we pray] 'and to humble' (make *lowly*) the wicked."

the part. Consequently, the *"Alter"* of Slabodka[4] preached for decades about the greatness of man. Likewise, our Sages also tell us not to *consider* ourselves wicked,[5] lest we indeed *become* wicked.

Similarly, to improve our children's behavior, we must improve their self-image. Unfortunately, however, we tend to notice only when things go wrong.[6] For instance, teachers often react immediately to misbehavior, even taking pride in catching children "red-handed." Similarly, business managers intent upon "increasing efficiency" keep an eagle eye open for any employee who functions at a mere 90% of his full capacity. Instead of praising a worker who is performing at 90% of his capacity, employers demand the other 10%.

Parents, too, are often too busy to notice their child unless he's being difficult. Thus, a teacher can go a whole school year without hearing from certain parents; only when their child's grades slip or a behavioral problem crops up do these parents suddenly speak up. We rarely take the few

---

4. Known as the *"Alter"* of Slabodka, Rav Nosson Tzvi Finkel, *zt"l* (1849-1927) was among the most gifted mentors in recent Jewish history. His more famous disciples include Rav Aharon Kotler, Rav Yaakov Kaminetsky, and Rav Yitzchok Ruderman, זכרונם לברכה.
5. See *Pirkei Avos* 2:13.
6. See the Vilna Gaon's commentary on *Brochos* 8a, where he points out that we become used to happiness but never misfortune. His example is marriage: When someone marries a woman of valor, he thinks of her in the past tense, as it says; "One who *found* a [good] woman *found* goodness..." (Mishlei 18:22). In contrast, when referring to a wicked woman the present tense is used: "I *find* the woman more bitter than death...." (Koheles 7:26). This is because we become so accustomed to good fortune that we remember it only as something that once happened to us, whereas suffering remains in its vivid, present reality.

moments necessary to inform teachers that our child is excelling or at least improving, nor do we thank them for a job well done.

No wonder our children need lots of discipline: *They unconsciously prefer parental disapproval to parental indifference.*

As parents, we have to walk a thin line. On one hand, we are the people best equipped to see our children's weaknesses and try to strengthen them. On the other hand, both we and our children must appreciate their many wonderful traits, for the recognition of these qualities is crucial to a happy and successful life.

So for every fault you find in your child, find a virtue. This habit will prevent overreaction and ensure that any necessary criticism will be presented calmly and kindly.

> *A father consulted me regarding his five-year-old son, who would return from school each day and complain about his teacher. My advice was to listen to his child's complaints provided that with each point of criticism which he voiced, he would also have to point out something that the teacher had done right. After several days the child realized that his teacher, like everyone else, had positive and negative attributes and no longer felt that his teacher was "terrible."*

In addition, praise your child sincerely and often. Even low-keyed but frequent plaudits can make him want to live up to your high opinion of him. Make sure your expectations are realistic, however, as the following true story teaches us:

> *Yossie, a teenager, consulted me about an emotional problem, one that had been plaguing him as long as he could remember. He had always been disappointed in himself. During our discussion, the fact emerged that when*

he was very young, his father had told him that before Yossie's birth he had dreamt he would have a child who would "light up the world." Ever since, any misbehavior or underachievement on Yossie's part had left him feeling like a failure, that perhaps he would fail to fulfill his father's dream.

The unique problems faced by children of highly successful parents are also widespread and well-known. Difficulties develop when these children are expected to follow in their parents' illustrious footsteps. Such parents should bear in mind a few simple guidelines:

First, resist the impulse to harp on your children's responsibility to carry on where their forebears left off.

One student of mine bore the name of his illustrious grandfather, a world-renowned Torah sage. Whenever this child misbehaved, he was reprimanded with the words "Now does this befit someone whose name is..."

Second, recognize that your child may not be *meant* to play the role you envision for him. Differentiate between your dreams and his reality, and there will be less tension surrounding his difficulties in fulfilling your ambitions. Indeed sometimes these setbacks indicate that he is unsuited to that calling. *Remember, your child is a sacred trust from Hashem, to be guided along whatever unique road is to his own benefit.*

Many people disdain pre-ordained paths, preferring to carve a niche for themselves of their very own. So if you want your children to succeed in their own way, help them realize two important ideas:

First, they can *surpass* their forebears. Hashem measures success in many ways. In each generation, a family's success can manifest itself differently. For instance, someone whose father was a great teacher of Torah can still be proud of a child who becomes an even greater scholar in one area, such as Halacha. Such a child should treasure his lineage,[7] but it should be an asset and an encouragement, not a burden.

Second, a child can, *and sometimes should,* find his own variation on the theme begun by his parents or grandparents. For example, a family priding itself on its Torah scholarship can also be proud of a child who successfully reaches out to Jews who are far from Judaism, something unheard of among his ancestors.

> *The story is told of a child of a great Chassidic dynasty whose home had been destroyed by fire. When his mother lamented the illustrious family tree that had been lost to the flames, he comforted her by promising to begin an equally great family tree.*

In Summary

- Children require more praise than criticism.
- Children should be encouraged to find their own path in life, while guided in the Torah path.

---

7. Indeed, all of *Klal Yisroel* is royalty; see *Bava Kamma* ch. 8, mishna 6 and *Bava Metzia* ch. 7, mishna 1.

13

Staying Afloat

Disciplining your child can often be painful because it can mean denying him what he wants and thinks he deserves. You love your child and hate to disappoint him, so you suffer along with him whatever he must endure as consequence of his misbehavior.

Parents instinctively protect their children from pain, and must often act as buffers during times of crisis. People remember their mother and father best for the comfort they provided during an especially trying period. Their solace, support, and security make an indelible imprint on a child's impressionable soul.

The reverse also holds true, and perhaps to an even greater extent. If a parent was *not* there when needed, the child remembers this and may conclude that he or she was not truly loved. Parents themselves have such memories, good and bad, about their own parents, so their desire to spare their own child is not only instinctive and emotional but also intellectual and calculated. After all, they don't want *their* child to feel unloved and abandoned, and they certainly don't want him to have bad memories of *them*.

It is therefore understandable that many parents withhold

discipline, finding it too difficult. Furthermore, they frequently mitigate any unfortunate consequences of their child's misbehavior at school or among his peers. They become his "defenders" against "unfair" teachers and friends. Sometimes these "outsiders" do treat their students or friends unjustly, but it is often the child's own character flaws which brought on other people's unpleasant reactions. Thus, when he clashes with a teacher over poor study habits, it is often the first time an adult (and a respected one at that) has severely criticized him. At times like these, "protecting" him certainly will not help him mend his ways. Indeed, children even tend to get themselves into trouble because they know their parents always bail them out. Such parents are unwittingly encouraging their children's irresponsibility and immaturity.

We should, of course, give our children the moral support they deserve during these periods of crisis. They must know that we are always with them and ready to help however we can. But this does not mean that we will extricate them from problems that are consistently of their own making.

Unfortunately, sometimes a child most needs his parents' warmth and comfort precisely when they *mustn't* intervene. How, then, can parents develop the necessary resolve to respond firmly when necessary? Let's start with a true story.

> *A certain young child used to throw himself on the floor whenever his demands weren't met. He would hold his breath and begin turning blue, at which point his mother, fearing the worst, would invariably give in. This continued for some time. Finally, a good friend of the mother's convinced her that she was doing her son a disservice by allowing him to "blackmail" her. Physiologically there was no real danger, for even if the child should lose consciousness, he would automatically resume breathing. So the mother began refusing her son's demands. Soon, the boy*

ceased trying to dominate her in this way.

Before focusing on the main lesson to be gleaned from this story, it must be said that such an extreme attempt on the part of a young child to "get his way" certainly did not happen overnight. After all, it isn't easy or pleasant to hold your breath until you turn blue. Perhaps this was an act of desperation on the part of the child to try and get his mother's attention after all else had failed. When it worked, the child continued to use it. What he needed was loving attention, not discipline, but he also had to be weaned from such drastic means of getting his way.

We can now ask: What enabled this mother to disregard her anxiety about her "suffocating" child? It was the realization that he would suffer *more* by learning, consciously or unconsciously, to manipulate others, especially those closest to him. The *same* maternal love and concern that initially caused her to "give in" gave her the strength to refuse his unjust demands.

We all have feelings. It's part of being human. The *Shem MiShmuel* likens the heart (the emotions) to the moon and the mind (the intellect) to the sun, for emotions wax and wane, just like the moon, while the intellect remains stable, like the sun. He calls them the two beacons that light up our inner selves just as the sun and moon illuminate our outer world.[1]

---

1. See *Shem MiShmuel*, Vayikra, p. 361, and Bereishis, vol. 2, p. 276. These two parts of the psyche also represent the Jewish people's two dynasties: the House of Ephraim and the House of David. Like the intellect, Ephraim's father, Yosef, remained constant. He was the same *tzaddik* in Egypt as he was in his father's house. David, on the other hand, symbolized the emotions, with his spirituality fluctuating like his forefather Yehudah's (see Bereishis 38). At the

Sometimes, however, we experience harmful emotions such as envy, hatred, greed, or unproductive anxiety. The fact that the Torah prohibits these emotions[2] is indicative of the damage they can do to us and to others. Yet, repressing these feelings doesn't work; in fact, it usually intensifies them. As the *Michtov MeEliyahu* notes, as important as suppressing the evil inclination may be, it is like pressing down on a coil: The more force you apply, the more forcefully the coil will spring back.[3]

This would seem to suggest that repression *alone* can eventually bring extremely negative consequences. It is best, therefore, to deal with these feelings by either *redirection* or *substitution*.

"Redirection" means that an emotion is refocused, that the love you bear your child can fuel a wide variety of responses, but all of them indicate your love.[4] Imagine your child reaching for his third helping of sweets. Only your concern for his welfare allows you to firmly put limits on his indulgence. As our hapless mother realized, *because* she loved

---

time of Redemption, these two dynasties will unite, granting the Jewish people eternal happiness (see Yechezkel 37).

2. See *Tiferes Yisroel*, sec. 77, at the end of the first chapter of *Kiddushin*, where the author explains that few Torah commandments deal with character since the infinite variety of personalities and situations is beyond the confines of the Written Law. The *Gemora*, of course, discusses proper behavior at length.
3. See Rav E. E. Dessler, *Michtov MeEliyahu*, vol. 1, p. 235.
4. Divine justice and Divine mercy both stem from Hashem's benevolence. Thus, Rav Shlomo Wolbe, *shlita*, notes, "...[both] Your rod and Your staff comfort me" (Tehillim 23:4), even though only the staff supports whereas the rod punishes, we should not lose sight of the fact, however, that rod and staff are actually one and the same object, a piece of wood. So too does Hashem's mercy and His justice stem from one source — His benevolence.

her "suffocating" child, she had to disregard his wishes.

Yet you need not explain to your child that you are standing firm because you love him. He will quite likely reject this claim of love. After all, if you really loved him you would let him do as he pleased! Such resistance from your child makes it all the more difficult to follow through on your disciplinary action. Even worse, once your child asserts that you really don't care for him, he is apt to believe it.

"Substitution" means replacing one emotion with another. For example, instead of hating someone who is inconsiderate, it is instead possible to pity him, by thinking: "Poor character invariably causes so much unhappiness." Or, "People are likely to avoid him, he'll probably suffer marital strife," etc. Once you *feel sorry* for someone, you can overcome your hatred.

Similarly, imagine your child growing up to be unpleasant, selfish and undisciplined. How *ashamed* you would feel! Then, substitute your dread of disciplining him now with your dread of such embarrassment in the future.[5] But don't let either scenario overwhelm you to the degree that your emotions warp your judgment. Your emotions are meant to be your servants, empowering you to act when action is called for. They are not your master and they should not cause you to do or say things you may later regret.

Alternatively, imagine how your child would feel if, even as an adult, he were still throwing tantrums to get his way. Think how miserable his life would be. Out of compassion for

---

5. See Rav Yehoshua Heller, *Divrei Yehoshua*, sec. 2, ch. 2, where the author advises readers "to exchange one inclination for another." For example, he writes, should a volatile, stingy person become embroiled in a dispute, he can control his temper by projecting what it would feel like to be taken to court for his irrational behavior. It could cost him money! This can serve as a deterrent for behavior he might later regret.

him, you can then prevent this eventuality by disciplining him now.

Substitution lets you positively *rejoice* at being able to stop your child's misbehavior at a relatively young age. Imagine if you hadn't had the foresight to correct his behavior early on! The joy of giving the right "medicine" at the right time can help overcome the pain of the present. A stark example of this from my own experience comes to mind.

> *One Shabbos afternoon my one-year-old twins discovered an open bottle of coated pills which had been inadvertantly left by a guest. Some of the pills had already had their coating sucked off. We had no way of knowing how many pills had originally been in the container. Dr. Lafair, a neighbor, insisted after examining the pills that we immediately rush to the hospital. When we arrived at Shaarei Tzedek, the verdict was clear and grim. Their stomachs must be pumped, and immediately. They were on a Shabbos shift and understaffed. I was asked to hold down my son's hands while they inserted a tube down his nose and into his stomach. He never took his eyes off me. In pain and fear, he glared at me accusingly, as if to say, "I trusted you. I gladly let you take me here. Now look what they're doing to me. And you're even holding me down!" It was one of the worst moments of my life. But I was also overjoyed that my children were getting timely and competent treatment that would save their lives. It was this joy, as well as the seriousness of the moment, that spurred me to hold my son down ever more firmly.*

Look beyond the present and into your child's future. Your love and devotion will give you the strength to cope with the pain which all parents must endure for the sake of their children's future happiness.

I once heard the following story from a renowned

educator in Yerushalayim, Rav Gamliel Bottleman, *shlita*:

Some men were once smuggling contraband over the border in a casket, posing as mourners in a mock funeral. Eventually, however, one border guard noticed that no one was crying. "Strange," he thought. "A funeral with no tears." So he ordered the casket opened. Then everyone started to cry. Said the guard, "If you had cried earlier, you wouldn't have to cry now."

So, too, if we agonize a little over our children's upbringing, we'll avoid worse agony later.

In Summary

- *Redirect* emotions toward positive values.
- *Substitute* negative feelings for positive ones.

14

Letting Go

One of the greatest pleasures of parenting — and teaching — is watching your "student" grow, mature and even surpass you. As our Sages have taught us, "A man can be jealous of anyone, except for his child or student" (*Sanhedrin* 105b). After all, my child or student is an extension of myself, and his success is therefore mine as well.

Teachers want to see their charges become independent and incorporate what they've learned into their own decision-making. Thus, Moshe Rabbeinu did not consider himself dead as long as Yehoshua lived.[1] I think the reason for this is that when Yehoshua responded to a question, you could *be sure* that this would have been Moshe's response as well.[2]

---

1. See Rashi on Devorim 31:29.
2. I once heard from HaGaon Rav Chaim Shmuelevitz, *zt"l*, that he only derived pleasure from this world twice. First, he made a statement and was told that Rav Yeruchem Levovitz, *zt"l*, had said the same thing, then Rav Chaim knew he *was* a true student. Second, a student of his shared an original Torah thought, that dovetailed with one of Rav Chaim's ideas, then Rav Chaim felt the joy of knowing he *had* a true student.

Consciously or subconsciously, however, some parents have trouble "letting go." Indeed, parents in their eighties have been known to remind their sixty-year-old "children" to dress warmly on a chilly day.

Each of life's stages presents unique challenges.[3] Yet as Rav Shlomo Fisher, *shlita*,[4] once said, all the "*mazel tov*'s" of life have one common denominator. When a baby is born, its umbilical cord is useless and, since it must now exert itself to nurse, it now bears some of the responsibility for its own feeding. *Mazel tov*! Upon reaching maturity, he or she becomes responsible for fulfilling the Torah's commandments. *Mazel tov*! At marriage, new responsibilities are shouldered. Upon becoming a parent, one becomes even more accountable. *Mazel tov, Mazel tov*!

The Hebrew word for "responsibility," אחריות, is related to the word אחרית, end, for responsibility means being accountable for a situation's ultimate outcome. This demonstrates the relationship between responsibility and authority — one can't be responsible for something he can't control.

Some parents have difficulty increasing their children's authority over their lives. But it's human nature to want to manage one's own affairs. We never outgrow the need to ask *daas Torah* on a wide variety of issues, but we must also learn to stand on our own two feet.[5]

---

3. See *Koheles Rabbah* 1:2, which describes the "seven worlds" of development in a lifetime. Also see *Alei Shor*, vol. 2, p. 659, for a revealing treatment of this theme.
4. Rav Shlomo Fisher is a *rosh yeshiva* of Yeshivas Itri, Yerushalayim.
5. See Maharal, *Nesivos Olom, Nesiv HaTorah*, ch. 4, where the author writes:

...ורב חסדא אומר איזה שונא מתנות יחיה כי מי ששונא את המתנות
ראוי שיהיה בשביל זה חי, כי המקבל דבר מזולתו אין ראוי לו החיים כי
החי עומד בעצמו, ולפיכך אמרו כי העני נחשב כמת וזה מפני שאין לו
החיים בעצמו כאשר הוא צריך לזולתו ואין לו בעצמו החיים, אבל מי

Children are no exception. They want to be able to make decisions. Parents must teach their children how to make these decisions, with an eye to eventually "letting go." This often means allowing for mistakes, some are trivial, such as broken eggs when children are learning to make their own breakfast. Some may be more serious or costly. *But failure is a learning experience,* so be prepared for your children's inevitable errors.[6]

שהוא שונא מתנות שהוא רוצה שיהיה עומד בעצמו מבלי שיקבל מאחר ודבר זה הוא החיים, ולכן יקרא המעיין שהוא נובע בעצמו ולא קבל המים נקרא מעין חיים, כי חיותו בעצמו ואינו מקבל המים, ולפיכך אמר איזה שונא מתנות יחיה זה הרואה טריפה לעצמו שאינו חס על שלו כלל.

This idea complements the concept that we were placed in this world to choose correctly. Our ability to do so is the essence of human life. This independence necessitates an "apprenticeship," however, when a young person learns from those older and wiser than he how to make decisions. Parents are his first guides; as such, they essentially prepare him for life.

6. See *Be'er Mechokek* (pp. 203-4) where the author, Rav Mordechai Katz, zt"l (1894-1964) *rosh yeshiva* of Telz Yeshiva, notes that G-d allowed the Jewish people to spy out Canaan even though He knew there would be dire consequences:
"...the Torah teaches us that although one can sometimes teach and express an opinion about a certain action or trait, nonetheless sometimes one cannot prevent the public or individual from performing a certain action, even though its faultiness is evident, for when it is palpably clear that reproof will not be accepted, for whatever reason, and should one restrain [the people or person in question], it could have the opposite effect. It is therefore one of the principles of education not to prevent the implementation of this course of action until [the persons] themselves can understand their mistake. Regarding this, it is said that just as it is a mitzva to say something that will be heard, it is a mitzvah not to say something that will not

Hard to Let Go

There are several understandable reasons why parents find it hard to relinquish control over their children's lives, even gradually.

First of all, most of us want to be needed. However, as wonderful as it is to give to others who really need you, it's another thing altogether to hold on just to be needed. Remember, your life experience is greater than your child's, so if your relationship is healthy and you "let go" wherever he can manage on his own, he will still consult you in other areas. This will certainly occur if you yourself set an example by turning to others when necessary.

Another reason we don't "let go" easily is that we want to shield our children from the painful consequences of wrong decisions. But they must learn that mistakes — and their price — are to be expected; it's part of their preparation for life. *Mistakes can have unpleasant consequences, but fear of making mistakes is worse.* So equip your children to make reasonable decisions, then reassure them that most blunders are neither irreparable nor tragic.

Some parents fear "losing" their children if they become too independent. Actually, the reverse is true. When you "let

---

be heard (*Yevamos* 65b)."

Thus, the *Ribono Shel Olom* understood that preventing the spies' mission would have been worse than allowing it. (Generally, of course, a parent must restrain his child from dangerous actions, even if a parent-child confrontation will develop. As *Mori VeRabi, zt"l,* put it, a child before bar mitzva has no *yetzer tov* (good inclination). How can a person live without a *yetzer tov*? *Mori VeRabi* answered that the parent is the *yetzer tov*. However, the *Ribono Shel Olom* understood that it would have been a mistake to prevent the Jews from dispatching the spies, and therefore He consented.)

go," children consult you *more*, for they know you won't make the decision for them, or impose your viewpoint. Their turning to you under such circumstances is, in fact, a sign of their growing *strength*, since they are asking you of their own volition.

A wise Jew once explained to me that his sons-in-law seek his advice because *he never volunteers it*, even though he is renowned for his sound counsel. He never expresses opinions about their family life. Sometimes they approach him, saying: "Make believe we are strangers. What would you advise us about such and such a problem?" Once, when his newlywed daughter asked him about a matter of *hashkafah*, he directed her to her husband. This father's "letting go" is a sign of his strength, and it is precisely why his sons-in-law do not view him as a threat to their stature in their own homes.

If parents don't let go, emotionally healthy children will pull away. I advise parents who study with their children to stop five minutes *before* your child needs to stop. Let him stretch his legs or begin another activity. That way, he'll look forward to his next study session.

Role-Modeling Asking for Advice

To sum up, don't forget that you must prepare your children to live successfully on their own. This involves letting them gradually take more and more control over their own lives. If, both as a part of your *chinuch* and by personal example, you teach them by example that it's wise to consult others when confronted by thorny problems, then they will have an excellent chance to live properly and successfully. Your good relationship with them will remain intact, since they've learned that consulting others, including parents, makes good sense.

Waiting Until They're Ready

The idea that people pass through many stages of life is important to us in understanding yet another potential cause of disciplinary problems. For just as parents musn't hold on too long and too tightly to their children, neither must they let go before their youngsters are emotionally or intellectually ready (although relinquishing control too late can be more problematic than doing so too soon). Regarding the danger of imposing more discipline than a child's age warrants, Rav Shlomo Wolbe,[7] *shlita*, explains:

> Just as it is impossible to eradicate natural tendencies of character, it is impossible to ignore a child's developmental stages. In vain do zealous mothers toil to accustom their children to matters that, by virtue of their age, should not yet become issues. *Even if such parents succeed* [emphasis mine], they may actually harm their child! It should be clear: Any demand that is incongruous with a child's age is liable to wound his tender heart, a wound which can in the future have a worrisome effect on his development and personality. This [effect] can find expression in the form of fears, nervousness, and lack of independence at an age that demands independence. (These words refer even to such simple matters as [an insistence on] cleanliness, sitting in an orderly fashion around the table, etc., as mothers customarily demand of their children several years before the appropriate time.)
> *Alei Shur*, vol. 1, p. 263

---

7. One of today's great Torah educators, Rav Shlomo Wolbe, *shlita*, lives in Eretz Yisroel and is the author of the widely acclaimed two-volume work *Alei Shur*.

In short, you must know *when* and *when not* to insist on certain behavior.

Many parents rightly impose a curfew on their children. However, your child may resent your insistence on matters considered "babyish" by environmental or social standards. For example, his friends may not have curfews. Or perhaps they smoke, etc. So if you want your child to adhere to your values rather than those around him, take time *early* to establish a special relationship with him — or don't raise him where you're raising him. The following true example puts this idea into focus:

> *A student of mine once considered stopping his child, growing up in the United States, from playing baseball, considering it a symbol of the dominant culture from which he wanted to protect his son. I felt that without a very good reason, such a request was unreasonable, given his country and circumstances.*

Likewise, your child may correctly feel that the time has arrived for him to make judgments on matters that were previously a parental prerogative, bedtime, eating habits, etc. Your insistence on maintaining complete control over such questions can cause recurrent, bitter conflict.

You must prepare yourself and your child for the time when you're going to be "letting go." This transfer in decision-making should be made *before* your child demands it; this way, he won't consider it a sign of weakness to ask your advice afterwards, since you're the one who gave him the reins.

It follows, therefore, that if you constantly find yourself battling with him over the same matter over a long period of time, then it may be a sign that your child is either not yet ready to shoulder certain responsibilities or is already past the stage when such control is appropriate. So take a careful look at your child before making demands of him. Is he developmentally ready? Can he *comprehend* what you want? Are your expectations premature?

If you're not sure, let go. Forgo the discipline.

In Summary

• Part of parental responsibility is to help children become capable of functioning independently.
• Be their role-model for seeking advice. Your children are like to emulate you.
• Make sure you transfer responsibility to your child at his proper developmental stage.

15

Watching Your Health

People tend to overlook the obvious. Novelties catch our eye and engage our mind. We often fail to appreciate what we've always had, taking for granted those things that are so vital to our happiness.

In his introduction to the *Mesillas Yesharim* (The Path of the Just), Rav Moshe Chaim Luzzato, *zt"l*, when referring to the great truths of life, puts it this way:

> ...I have not written this work to teach men what they do not know...for you will find in most of my words only things that most people know and do not doubt. *But to the degree that they are well known and their truths self-evident, so too is it quite common for them to be forgotten* [emphasis mine].

Because of this tendency to forget, the more important the idea, the more the Creator, in His mercy, makes this knowledge available. As Rav Tzodok HaKohen writes:

> All worldly matters as well as all the world's creatures remind man that there is a Creator...as I have heard it explained with regard to the verse "...all the world is

Your possession," [Tehillim 104:24] this means that each day Hashem summons for man various things that can remind [him] to remember the Creator. For this reason, our Sages instituted blessings for all physical pleasures, such as food, vision and hearing...for good news and its opposite, for clothing, etc.

Tzidkas HaTzaddik, sec. 232

One of the most prominent aspects of the animal world is the drive for self-preservation. Once again we turn to Rav Tzodok:

It is the nature of all creatures to flee from that which harms them, *and from this we are taught to use our free will to guard the body and refrain from harmful activities even with regard to mitzvos* [emphasis mine].

Ibid., sec. 173

We tend to take our health for granted, even though preserving it is not only a positive commandment[1] but is also the basis of all spiritual accomplishment.

---

1. *Sefer HaChinuch*, mitzva 546:
Man must protect himself from common phenomena, for G-d created His world and built it on the pillars of nature, decreeing that fire should burn and water should quench the flame. Similarly, nature decrees that if a large stone falls on a person's head, his brain will be crushed, and if a person falls from a high roof, he will die. The Creator, blessed be He, graced human bodies and blew into [each of] them a living soul, which knows how to protect the body from injury...and since G-d has subjugated man's body to (the forces of) nature, as His wisdom dictated ([the body] being physical), He commanded him (his mind) to guard against [harmful] occurrences. Since he is at the mercy of nature, it will wreak its effects on him if he does not guard against it.

While visiting Lithuania, one of Yerushalayim's great men asked Rav Yisroel Salanter how to improve his character. Rav Yisroel answered, "There is no greater ingratitude to Hashem than to abuse the body He gave to you."[2]

Poor health also distorts our judgment. Indeed, when people who seem overwhelmed by their grievances approach *Mori VeRabi* HaGaon Rav Chaim Pinchus Scheinberg, *shlita*, he sometimes tells them *"Gei shloff zich oyse"* (Go get some good sleep). A rested person has a different perspective on the world. Thus, the *Halacha obligates* teachers of young children to go to bed early.[3] Teachers need to be in full possession of all their faculties in order to give their students what they need and deserve.

If this is true for teachers, then parents would certainly profit from paying closer attention to their health. At least teachers have a respite each night from the problems they encounter in the classroom. Furthermore, they are not as personally involved in the often turbulent process of growing up. They are nonetheless enjoined to get a good night's sleep. How much more so do parents need to get proper rest! Even simply resting in a dark room can revitalize you almost as much as sleep. Ten or fifteen minutes is of great value; it needn't be an hour or two.

It's so obvious, yet so neglected. Proper sleep and diet are important for maintaining a balanced attitude towards problems. Situations which loom large and unsolvable take on a different perspective after proper sleep. Keeping away from foods rich in sugar, caffeine or other stimulants help a person avoid mood swings that disrupt the decision-making process.

---

2. *BeTuv Yerushalayim*, by the *maggid* Rav Ben Tsiyyon Yadler, *zt"l*, p. 342.
3. See *Rama, Shulchan Oruch, Yoreh Deah* 245:17.

These foods can cause us to overreact to our children, and to do or say things which we might later regret.

The best time to rest or eat something light and nutritious is right before "rush hour," i.e., immediately before your children (or your spouse!) return home. It's best to face their demands for your immediate attention with a well-rested mind.

So, it is essential to control sleep patterns and to monitor your diet. You will approach problems more realistically, and solve them more effectively.

In Summary

- You must be healthy in order to function properly as a parent.
- Good nutrition and sleep habits help keep you healthy.

16

Reward and Punishment

Whenever the subject of discipline comes up, people invariably speak of "reward and punishment." However, since we react sooner to misbehavior than to good conduct, "crime and punishment" would be a more appropriate term for these discussions. But remember, although any effective disciplinary system makes some provision for punishment, it must be understood that the need to implement the punishment is a symptom of the *failure* of that system. An effective disciplinary system revolves around three ideas:

First, a child must know that misbehavior often *will* be punished, or at least there is a clear potential for punishment.

Second, once your child can understand cause and effect, your punishment must be a fair one.

Third, punishment should as a rule not be harsh. There are several reasons for this. Everyone knows that a really harsh punishment is likely to produce resentment, which hardly wins you a disciple. Furthermore, when you threaten a particularly harsh punishment, you often back down, undermining the credibility of a future warning. You then portray yourself to your child as someone who threatens but doesn't carry through. Your credibility will suffer and your child is then tempted to "try his luck," hoping to get away with his misbehavior once again.

The Two Forms of Punishment

We find two types of punishment in the Torah. One type is called מדה כנגד מדה (measure for measure). For instance, when man couldn't correctly utilize the luxuries of Gan Eden, Hashem saw that this situation was not good for him. So, in His infinite mercy, the Master of the World relegated man to a land which would produce "thorns and thistles" (Bereishis 3:18).

This form of punishment generally spotlights the area where the recipient must improve. Thus, a toothache may point to a laxity in speech-oriented mitzvos or kashrus.

The other type of punishment manifests itself as a natural consequence of the sin. For example, Adam became mortal *as a result* of his eating from the Tree of Knowledge. Likewise, on a more mundane plane, a toothache can also result from the neglect of oral hygiene. The Creator wants us to care for our health, and tooth decay is the way Hashem shows His displeasure with someone lax in caring for his teeth.[1] Accordingly, the recipient of this form of punishment can reform himself by *tracing* his problems to his misbehavior.[2]

---

1. See *Igros Chazon Ish*, 35:

כי מה שאנו קורין טבע המכוון בזה רצון היותר מתמיד של המהוה כל
הויות יתברך...

For that which we call 'nature' refers to the most common expression of the desire of the Source of all existence, blessed be He. When people disregard their health they defy Hashem's wishes.

2. See *Aderes Eliyahu* on Bereishis 2:17. Also see Rav Elchonon

In interpersonal relationships the second type of punishment is usually the appropriate one (although if you cannot come up with a "natural" consequence of certain misbehavior, you must still react, remembering, of course, to be as fair, firm and friendly as possible). Actions cause reactions which can be connected and related to each other. As the Rambam points out, when you treat others well, you will in turn be treated kindly by them.[3] Conversely, inconsiderate people suffer from their inconsiderate behavior more than anyone else. As the *Gemora* says, "the angry person remains only with his anger," i.e., his temper gains him nothing but ill health.[4]

Parents must prepare their children for adulthood, when they will be held responsible for their actions. Therefore, it would be unwise to constantly protect your children from the consequences of their misdeeds. To consistently shelter them is to give them a poor preparation for life. Allowing them to be rude to you or to excuse their rudeness to others will result in their rudeness going unchecked. Later on in life, this will cause your child untold sorrow. Not only will your child

---

Wasserman, *zt"l*, at the end of "*Maamar Al HaTeshuva*," where he quotes the *Ran*.

Another example of these two punishments is found in *Megillah* 15b: When the Divine Presence left Esther as she entered Achashverosh's idol-filled anteroom, she could have ascribed this departure to the unnatural consequence that the *Shechina* doesn't rest in places where there are idols (see Rashi on *Shemos* 9:29). Instead, however, she realized that she was being punished, measure for measure, for speaking disrespectfully of King Achashverosh (calling him a "dog," see Tehillim 22:21 and *Megillah* 15b), thereby causing the King of the World to remove His presence from her.

3. *Peah* 1:1.
4 See *Kiddushin* 41a and Rashi ad loc.

suffer through poor relationships throughout life, but will feel that people are "unfair" or "too sensitive" when in fact he has simply never learned to treat others with the respect due them.

It has often been said that punishment should fit the crime. This means that your child becomes aware, through the consequences that he incurs with his misbehavior, that what he does will cause other things to occur. For example, going to bed late can lead to oversleeping the next morning, arriving late at school, and upsetting one's teacher or principal. Likewise, failure to clean one's room results in an inability to find things, and not putting soiled clothes in the hamper means that the supply of clean clothes will run out. A mother who haggles with her child to get to bed on time or gives him a note excusing his lateness is not doing him any favor (especially since this parent is role modeling lying!), nor is a parent who tidies up her children's room or picks up their dirty clothes off the floor helping prepare him for adulthood. (The revered *tzaddik*, Reb Aryeh Levine, *zt"l*, when asked by his soon-to-be-wed grandson for advice on building a happy home, responded by telling him to remember not to leave his socks on the floor!) Unquestionably, you must not demand of your children what is beyond their level of maturity and understanding. But it is just as wrong to shield them from responsibility once they mature. The best policy is that of the parent in the following story:

> *Late for school as usual, Shimon asks his mother for a note saying that he wasn't feeling well that morning and was delayed. Mother replies that she will gladly write a note stating that since Shimon neglected to go to bed on time, he got up late this morning. Shimon refuses the note but gets to bed earlier that evening.*

Mitzvos Between Man and G-d

When training a child to observe the mitzvos between man and G-d, the "natural consequence" approach would seem inapplicable, since the consequences of sinning against G-d are generally less immediate than the repercussions of sinning against man. At second glance, however, we can see that this is not true, for discipline vis-à-vis mitzvos between man and G-d depends on two factors:
1. Your relationship with your child.
2. How you yourself view these mitzvos: Are they a burden or a joy and a privilege?

The most natural consequence of sinning against Hashem is that you distance yourself from Him. Just as the greatest reward is closeness to Him, so too the greatest punishment is the barrier erected by transgressions.

As a parent, you are Hashem's representative in this world. That's why — as Rav Yehoshua Freilich, *shlita*, points out — the *Gemora* says that parental honor is comparable to the honor of Hashem Himself.[5] Wherever parents are mistreated, Hashem is certain that He, too, would not have been treated properly had He lived there.[6] After all, His representatives are not treated respectfully. Divine displeasure is our worst punishment, just as parental displeasure should be a child's worst punishment for neglecting mitzvos. So if we want our children to remain loyal to Judaism, we must be *exceedingly careful* to maintain a warm, positive relationship with them. Only then will our dissatisfaction make an impression upon them.

In contrast, if we are harsh or overbearing, especially in enforcing Torah observance, we will defeat our own purpose. Our children will resent the Torah, G-d forbid, seeing in it an

---

5. See *Sanhedrin* 49b.
6. See *Kiddushin* 31a.

extension and symbol of our authoritarianism. Indeed, there has been a historical pattern showing that when parents were domineering toward their children, the latter have abandoned Torah. Sometimes it may be necessary to mete out punishment for a child's failure to keep mitzvos, but this should be the exception, not the rule. Your displeasure should be the greatest deterrent.

Torah observance should be a pleasure for *us*. When children love us and *see our joy of keeping the Torah,* they will be able to withstand exposure to an environment which runs counter to Torah ideals. As Rav Moshe Feinstein, *zt"l*, remarked, the generation of parents who felt that it was *"shver tsu zein a Yid,"* difficult to be a Jew, inadvertently discouraged their children from following such a "difficult" path.[7] Torah Jews are a minority. *Being different can be either a source of pride or a mark of shame to be discarded as soon as possible.* When children see that their Torah-true home is a place where they want to be, they identify with your values and will want to build such a home for themselves when they marry. So create a warm, caring relationship with your children, and they will, G-d willing, carry on the Torah way of life and gladly pass it on to their children.

---

7. See *Reb Moshe: The Life and Ideals of HaGaon Rabbi Moshe Feinstein* (Brooklyn: Mesorah Publications, 1986), p. 73, and *Dorash Moshe, Vayetzei,* pp. 22-23.

According to the Vilna Gaon in *Aderes Eliyahu,* Bereishis 3:1, one major claim of the evil inclination is that the Torah is impossible to observe. Parents must therefore combat this idea by showing the *joy* of mitzvos. For when we love something, even its difficulties are no burden.

Avoid Hitting

What we've said until now is that punishments shouldn't be arbitrary or overly harsh. Such measures can more accurately be termed retaliation. They don't work.

For this reason hitting is rarely appropriate. For it teaches your child that might makes right — and someday he'll be mightier than you. It also makes your child feel that you haven't thought through your reactions, You've merely lashed out. These perceptions will breed disrespect at best and open rebellion at worst.

> I once asked Rav Shlomo Wolbe, *shlita*, about hitting children. He responded that nowadays when you hit a three-year-old *he hits you back.*

The Torah forbids us to cause others to sin. Therefore, *halacha* prohibits parents from hitting older children, lest they sin by hitting back.[8] Rav Wolbe is telling us, then, that today even a three-year-old is considered an "older child."

Even aside from this angle, one thing is certain: When physical punishment is administered in anger or haste, it is bound to be detrimental. For most of us, this fact precludes the use of corporal punishment, for if we step back and take a hard look at the situation, we can usually think of a better solution than inflicting physical pain on our children.

Our Relationship with Our Children

In mitzvah education, whether mitzvos between man and G-d or interpersonal relationships, our "chemistry" with our children is vital.

---

8. See *Shulchan Oruch, Yoreh Deah*, 140:20.

When expressing your disapproval, shock or disappointment at your child's behavior, you can sometimes couple these emotions with *temporary* withdrawal of your closeness and support by asking him to *temporarily* stay away because *right now* you're too disappointed. Express clearly that you need a *finite* amount of time (*ten minutes or less*) to get over your disappointment.

This form of punishment is highly effective *provided that*:

1. Your relationship with your child is generally warm, giving and supportive.

2. You don't do it too often — even once a month is too much.

3. It has worked in the past, i.e., your child has felt badly about your disappointment.

If it hasn't worked — *stop using it!* Otherwise, you can permanently damage your relationship, which is probably already in trouble if your child is unaffected by parental withdrawal and disapproval. This could be the harbinger of many worse problems in the offing, for it's a sign that your connection and interaction with your child is negative or at best weak.

Giving Encouragement

Until now we've discussed how to deal with misbehavior through punishment. There is, however, a better way than punishing, at least most of the time. *While it is true that you need to deal with negative behavior, it's even more important to encourage good behavior.* This holds true especially when you want your child to improve his behavior in areas in which he has been lax up till now.

Some parents offer prizes for good conduct. My *mashgiach,* Rav Zvi Feldman, *zt"l,* of Mirrer Yeshivah in Brooklyn, quoted Rav Yeruchem Levovitz, *zt"l,* as saying that prizes should not be enjoyed by only one child. Children must be taught the joy of *giving*. Accordingly, part of the child's prize should be the knowledge that his good behavior benefits others, perhaps in the form of a treat he distributes to his siblings or friends.

In general, however, too many sweets should be avoided. As *Mori VeRabi* HaGaon Rav Chaim Pinchus Scheinberg, *shlita*, says, parents should not offer sweets too often as an incentive for good behavior. Too many sweets can be conducive to the development of a personality which is geared to pleasure-seeking, especially in the realm of physical gratification. Toys or games are therefore preferable, especially since they can be shared.

Private time with you is another incentive for good behavior. A walk or short trip with you gives your child the recognition he so deserves and needs. *It is far better to reward your children with your attention than to punish them by removing your closeness to them. Children need parents.*

Sometimes, following a designated period of good behavior, certain privileges can be granted, such as permission to buy something special in the neighborhood grocery, or a visit to a friend in a different neighborhood. Such rewards teach children about "cause and effect" in a positive way. Your message is clear: The more you behave like a grown-up, the more we can treat you like a grown-up. The implementation of such an approach will obviously vary with your child's age and inherent ability to properly utilize his newly acquired prerogatives.

Monitoring Improved Behavior

Any program which is based upon rewarding positive changes in behavior must have specific monitoring. What we mean by "monitoring" is a system where you child's progress is recorded. Success breeds success. Your child's progress will motivate him to continue and even increase his efforts, increasingly believing in his ability to change himself for the better.

In my experience, children have a good idea of what constitutes decent behavior. In addition, like everyone else, they yearn for the good feeling that comes when their parents approve of them. When children can be shown, through some sort of monitoring, that they are getting closer and closer to winning this approval, their improvement accelerates.

In addition, the monitoring clarifies whether there really has been a change for the better. This will help prevent children and parents from squabbling on this point.

Monitoring methods vary. Some parents spend a few minutes with their child every evening, talking about how the day has gone and recording their conclusions in some sort of diary. This method has the advantage of privacy, since some children don't want others, even (or especially) siblings, to know about their progress or lack of it. This private time is itself a powerful incentive for your child, because it will be so much more pleasurable if parent and child can agree that the day was a productive one, and allow the day to end on a note of parental approval and encouragement.

Charts — Some Specifics

Many families chart their children's improvement. A chart is, in effect, a *visual* record of your child's progress. Children are often highly visual, so seeing how they are doing can have a great impact on them.

Charts have other important advantages. A chart can pinpoint progress with stars or points introduced to emphasize this progress.

One of the biggest advantages of a chart system is that

it makes "time together" with your child a regular part of your schedule. Sometimes busy parents never "get around" to spending time with their children, but the chart provides you with a joint project. Each evening a few minutes are consistently set aside for reviewing the day's behavior and giving your child appropriate encouragement. One of the great benefits of this may be that even after the need for the chart is over, when his behavior is already fine, those moments together will be cherished and the habit of getting together will continue, only instead of being devoted to improving conduct, the time can now be used to talk. Talk about your child's fears and frustrations, talk about the happy things that happened that day. The more you give your children the opportunity to talk to you, the more they feel understood and the more likely they are to become your disciple.

Such daily meetings also accustom children in another supremely important area. Judaism places great stress on the value and need for *cheshbon hanefesh*. This "accounting of the soul," when properly executed, is of inestimable value in successful living. *Properly* done means *positively* done, i.e., an accounting that casts a generally positive light on one's behavior. Instead of dwelling on how badly this day has gone and projecting renewed failure for the next one, a person can focus on how to correct his mistakes and to take encouragement from the day's successes. For someone who tends to focus on the negative, each remembered failure from the day's events must also be accompanied by the memory of some positive accomplishment. This way, a person becomes aware of the direction his life is taking.

Use your daily review of the chart to teach your child how to focus on and evaluate his day, emphasizing his successes. This will help your child see his good points on his own. This is of immense importance. *Living as we do in a society which knows how to be critical but is often stingy with its praise, we have to learn how to encourage ourselves.* Relying on others for encouragement can be disappointing at best. There are several keys to an effective chart. First, a chart must be *specific*. For example, "being good" is too vague and subjective a chart heading, as is "helping out." Sometimes children will maintain that they've been "good" while according to you their behavior was far from acceptable. Such conversation will only foster disagreements and spoil your time together with your child. Even "speaking respectfully" is open to interpretation. "Speaking softly" or "saying please" (and meaning it!) is much better.

Second, don't overcrowd your chart. Even adults can't focus on too many things at once, and a long list of goals can easily discourage a child from even trying to improve.

Some positive behavior must be included on the chart at all times. Remember: you want to train your child to focus positively on himself. "Helping out" isn't specific enough, but "Helping dress the baby" is a good example of focusing on something positive.

Your chart should look something like the following:

	Sun.	Mon.	Tues.	Wed.	Thurs.	Fri.	שבת
Yankel							
Cleaning up toys							
Getting up by 7:15 with one reminder							
Dressing the baby							

Charts, from my experience, are generally effective until about age 10. Consequently, the rewards that the chart promises should not be scheduled in the too-distant future, for younger children will not be consistently motivated by the prospect of even a big prize if its realization is too far off. To keep up his spirit, it is much better to offer smaller prizes at frequent intervals.

An effective approach combines both on-the-spot encouragement and the greater allure of a bigger, more special prize: when a certain number of rewards have been won for short-term successes, then a substantial one is granted for the long-term progress.

This is actually training your child in an important principle for successful living: *We attain long-term goals primarily by achieving short-term goals.* Not only do short-term successes add up, the encouragement derived from achieving them enables people to successfully pursue the longer-range, formidable challenges.

It is also important to bear in mind that a reward is a reward only if it is something the person wants.[9] So plan out the rewards together with your child. Of course you must set limits, but offer *choices* of prizes and let your child do the choosing. A small prize can be something along the lines of a colorful eraser. Children like to collect erasers of various shapes and colors. Sets of tiny cars or (*lehavdil*) photographs of Gedolei Yisroel make ideal smaller prizes, since a child will want to expand his collection. This encourages ongoing good behavior.

Sometimes you want to reward children for a joint effort, such as getting along or cleaning up together. A family game or a short excursion can often motivate children to function better as a family.

One final point: Don't think that rewarding good behavior will mean trouble-free childrearing. Children are human, and we all have our ups and downs. Progress is often erratic,

---

9. See Rav Dessler, *Michtav Me'Eliyahu,* vol. 1, p. 17.

especially when tackling long-standing patterns. So don't become discouraged and don't discourage your children. Remind them that tomorrow is another day, that you're right behind them, believing in them and cheering them on. Knowing this is your child's greatest reward and inspiration.

In Summary

- Punishments should be a natural result of the misbehavior.
- Reward is far preferable to punishment.
- Monitor improved behavior.

17

How It Looks Doesn't Matter

How It Looks

As mentioned, "discipline" derives from the word "disciple." This means that the disciplinary process must be educational, i.e., geared *solely* toward your child's physical or emotional well-being. If you discipline him for any other reason, you can jeopardize his future as a parent, spouse, sibling, or as a well-functioning member of society. There are bound to be problems in his youth as well, as the following familiar scene best illustrates:

> *Yaakov, aged three, is in shul. As yet unable to read, he quickly grows restless and noisy. Yaakov's father, worrying over the disturbance his son is causing others, looks over at him with disgust and hisses "Shhh!" After a brief interlude, Yaakov starts up again, so his father "disciplines" him with a "potch," whereupon the child begins to howl and must be removed from shul.*

What's happening here? Yaakov's father is understandably worried about the disturbance his son is causing but aside from this, he was also *embarrassed* and *ashamed* by his son's behavior. What, then, was behind this father's "decision" to "discipline" his son? Does he calmly assess the situation, concluding that only by hitting his son can he "teach" him how to behave in shul, or is this father motivated by his own shame? After all, there were many people in shul who were witnessing *his child's* davening.

I've often seen a common variation of the above story: The father hits his small child and *the child hits him back*.[1] I once saw an amazing exchange, in which father and child hit each other *six times* before the father hit the "nuclear button" and gave his son a hard blow. The boy, of course, began to howl and the scene ended as it usually does, with the father hurriedly "evacuating" his child from shul.

Three points can be culled from this common scene: First, don't put your child into situations in which he's almost sure to misbehave. For instance, don't bring your child to shul until he can read, or at least identify the *aleph-beis*. This skill gives him something to do there, a feeling of participation, and a way to identify with what's going on around him. Consequently, when he matures, he will gain more from holy places, and better appreciate their sanctity. Furthermore, he won't have to unlearn bad habits. Certainly, even young children should be brought to shul so that they can absorb some of its *kedusha*, but these visits should be brief and conditional upon impeccable behavior. Indeed, any child who misbehaves in shul should be denied this privilege for the coming week. Furthermore, unruly children should not be taken to shul as a way of giving their mother some additional Shabbos morning rest. While she may truly need the rest, some other solution must be found.

Second, the use of physical punishment merely serves as

---

1. See p. 129.

a poor role model, teaching your child to solve his problems by force and by losing his temper. Just as breaking a promise to him trains him to be untruthful,[2] so too, hitting "educates" him to hit back, whether at you or at his siblings. On those rare situations when you have decided that a "potch" is indeed called for, it *must*, I repeat *must* be administered coolly, calmly, and with the clear implication that as a parent you have sorrowfully arrived at this regrettable conclusion. In addition, the child's resulting pain should stem more from the fact that you felt such action was necessary, rather than from the force of the blow.

Third, when we worry about appearances, our emotions get the better of us. Take our father-son examples: Had the child misbehaved at home, his father might have reacted more sensibly. Since he was concerned, however, with how *he* appeared to others, his emotions got the better of him. He forgot our most important rule: *Discipline must be solely for the recipient's benefit.*

As difficult as it may sometimes seem, we must ignore other people's opinions of us and our children. Focus only on what parental response best serves your child. Remember, onlookers forget, but your child may consciously or unconsciously resent your for years to come. And if this overreacting becomes a *pattern*, he certainly will not forget and probably will not forgive.

Your child is a sacred trust, so treat him accordingly. If you are concerned about onlookers, remember that Hashem is also looking on. All that matters is His opinion of how you handle your child's education.

---

2. See *Sukkah* 46b. See also p. 126.

In Summary

- Don't put your child in a position where he is likely to misbehave.
- Avoid corporal punishment.
- Your reaction to misbehavior must be determined by what your child needs, not by your embarrassment.
- *Discipline must be solely for the recipient's benefit.*

18

Keeping Your Cool

Our tremendous emotional attachment to our children serves as a powerful impetus for us to help them. We can spend many a night attending to a feverish child or a teething infant without feeling we deserve any special credit for it.[1] However, this incredible attachment with which we parents are blessed can also be our undoing. First of all, it can cause us to disregard warning signals. Indeed, even extremely competent educators can be blind to their own children's needs or shortcomings.

Second, our children's deficiencies can convince us that we've "gone wrong," leading us to find fault with both ourselves and our spouses. In the resulting emotionally charged

---

1. See *Tiferes Tziyon* on *Midrash Koheles* 1:1(b); ד״ה בן שנה דומה למלך.

"[The fact that a one-year-old resembles a king [with everyone fawning over him] is one of the kindnesses of the Creator, for were the love [for him] not so great, his father and mother would not have the strength to raise him, so enormous is the burden, for they neither rest by day nor enjoy any tranquility by night....

atmosphere, we are likely to say and do things we'll regret, with our children being the primary losers.

One of the simplest remedies for this problem is outside advice. If you're having doubts about your child's character development, consult a knowledgeable, objective teacher, principal, grandparent, friend, or neighbor. Parenting groups are also helpful, especially to fledgling parents, who need to learn that their problems are not unique and do not necessarily reflect on their own individual shortcomings.

Blaming yourself for your child's shortcomings is almost always counterproductive. Even when you *are* at fault, your guilt only immobilizes you or elicits behavior that you will later regret. Therefore, set aside guilt feelings, and attend to your child's needs as quickly and as correctly as possible.

Your Child Is a Sacred Trust

It helps enormously to realize that your child is not really *yours* but given to you as Hashem's trust. You can then be as objective as you would regarding someone else's child.

> *I once grappled with a difficult situation concerning one of my own children, until my wife asked me, "What would you tell someone else experiencing this problem?" Immediately, a solution came to mind.*

The Dangers of Negativity

Just as our intense emotional involvement with our children can blind us to their misbehavior or character flaws, it can make us exaggerate or imagine problems, to the point that we might often overlook our children's most wonderful virtues in the process.

Bear in mind this important point: *An inability to see our children's merits is worse than an inability to see their faults.*

Avoid Overreaction and Confrontation

Overreaction can create disciplinary problems by offending a child's sense of justice, thereby rendering him either confrontational or withdrawn. Whichever result is worse is of secondary importance, for one thing is clear: Whatever the child had said or done wasn't worth this aggravation.

While we must establish a clear behavioral code, confrontations should be avoided. For once a confrontation is under way, we must maintain our authority by resisting our children's pressure, lest it become an oft-used weapon. On the other hand, if we constantly win these "battles," our children can, G-d forbid, become embittered, unyielding, or indecisive, losing their sense of resolve along with the argument.

We see once again, as in chapter 3, that discipline involves three things:

fairness, firmness, and friendliness.

If you are too emotionally involved, you won't exhibit any of these traits. Firmness, if we are upset, easily turns to harshness, evenhandedness turns into its opposite, and as far as friendliness goes, an overwrought parent certainly doesn't seem very friendly. The resulting climate is certainly not conducive to proper discipline. Futhermore, when we consistently overreact or overpunish, we are headed for long-term trouble. We must therefore understand two things:

1. *Why* are we so excitable when it comes to our children?
2. What can we do about it?

The first question is easier to answer than the second. First, as stated, our self-image is often, and understandably, quite intertwined with our children's behavior, and how they are "turning out." We are also sensitive to what others think of us or our children; this factor can easily affect our judgment.

Frequently, in addition, we consider our authority threatened. Remember: Children *want* and *need* to look up to their parents, so our stature is rarely in danger (unless, of course, we overreact). To encourage our children's natural tendency to respect us, we must stay in control. Especially for younger children, an overly emotional parent can be frightening.

As for the second question, here are a few suggestions:

1. Project the Unexpected

We tend to lose our presence of mind when the unexpected happens. Therefore, as stressed in Chapter 3, anticipate any unavoidable emotional "showdowns" and prepare to be fair, firm, and friendly.

2. Take the Pressure Off of Yourself

No single inappropriate decision or response on your part will ruin your child the way constant overreaction will, so calm down. You can always subsequently announce that you've thought it over, or consulted others, and that you've changed your mind (especially if this change is to your child's liking!). This way, you show your child that there's nothing wrong with admitting mistakes and getting a second opinion. On the contrary, both demonstrate how much you care for him.

Sometimes, however, you mustn't reveal that you've consulted someone else, lest your child be embarrassed by hearing that you have revealed something he feels is a very private matter. Furthermore, it is certainly inadvisable to *constantly* change your mind.

So relax. Be less emotional and your decision is more likely to be correct.

3. Use Emotion Wisely

Some situations demand an emotional response. Indeed, if we always deal with our children calmly, they may feel unimportant compared to the things that do excite us.

So let yourself get emotional. But do so rarely, lest this technique lose its impact. Stay in control, no matter how agitated you seem. For what may begin as a "show" can soon become real, and that's dangerous. Therefore, exercise caution and wait until you are on top of the situation before trying any histrionics.

> *Rav Chaim Septimus, shlita, remembers how Rav Eliyahu Lopian, zt"l, the renowned mashgiach of the yeshivah in Kfar Chassidim, always used to say what he had heard in Kelm: As long as you still feel* כעס הלב, *internal anger, it's too early to use* כעס הפנים, *facial or pretended anger.*

4. Postpone Your Reaction as Well as Your Decision

Make a rule for yourself: Whenever you see a crisis brewing, do not mete out severe punishments or get embroiled in major confrontations until your spouse gets home. Aside from the importance of parents' making and acting on disciplinary decisions together (as discussed in Chapter 5), there is another reason to wait for your spouse:

When you become emotional, your spouse instinctively becomes calm. Admittedly, sometimes one frantic parent only upsets the other, but spouses often do counterbalance each other, and certainly should strive to do so.

Yet, when your spouse is upset by your child's behavior, don't act as if nothing has happened. *Back your husband or wife, but do so calmly.* When one spouse has the backing of the other then both can relax.

As for single parents, don't take major disciplinary action without first sleeping on it, consulting others, or both. The single parent must be even more circumspect and diplomatic with his/her children. The following true story, depicting an admittedly extreme situation, attests to the emotional investment a single-parent household requires:

Several rambunctious young orphans were raised by their sickly grandmother. Amazingly, their home atmosphere was always calm, and the children grew up to become fine adults. When asked how she accomplished this feat, the elderly lady said, "I never got myself into a confrontation, because I knew I'd then have to face the liveliness and the stubbornness of youth. Using distraction and humor, I avoided battles of wills."

Divorce and Remarriage

Divorce raises many complex child-raising questions. When a parent does not have custody of his children, his relationship with them is often delicate. Furthermore, great harm can be done to children who are caught between two parents who bear each other deep ill will.

When a divorcé remarries, the children's relationship with their stepparent affects not only the children themselves but the entire fabric of the new union. This situation is exacerbated if there are children from previous marriages on both sides. A healthy atmosphere must be created in the home, allowing each stepparent to assume a natural disciplinary role in an unnatural situation.

To ease these difficult transitions, I strongly urge that competent counseling be sought *before any problems crop up*. This way, they will not come as a surprise, nor will they be assumed to reflect negatively on the newly established home.

After all, these issues are part and parcel of an unfortunate turn of events. Powerful emotions will surface, and they must be understood and dealt with before they become masters of the situation.

Give Matters Proper Thought

Even when you feel the need to react in order to prevent a child's behavior from setting an example for his siblings, tell your children that you are giving the matter some thought. They'll learn that your reaction is indeed forthcoming. It often happens that during your deliberations, your child will simply apologize. You've both had time to think the matter over and can look at the situation with cooler heads.

In summary, our emotions are a powerful and *necessary* tool in our relationship with our children, but emotion can be both constructive and destructive, depending on whether we control it or it controls us.

---

2. See Rav Shamshon Raphael Hirsch, *Yesodos HaChinuch*, vol. 2, p. 53:
From his very first cry, the newborn expresses his "I want" or his "I do not want." He desires comfort and seeks to fend off discomfort. Weekly his desire grows, while his parents try as much as possible to fulfill his desire, until he becomes a dictator, ruling over his entire surroundings. Sometimes this [parental] surrender comes from too much coddling, and sometimes from a desire to silence his nerve-wracking screams in order that the parents can sleep in peace. *At any rate, this accustoms the child to the dangerous illusion that he need merely demand something and it will immediately be given to him; that he need merely upset those around him with his yelling and his will shall immediately prevail [emphasis mine].*

5. Daven

Last but certainly not least: No matter how perceptive you are, and how expert the advice you receive, you are *completely* dependent on Hashem's help. When asked for the secret of their success, innumerable parents pointed to their siddur or their Tehillim. As the Yiddish saying goes, "*meer tuen, Gott tut oof,*" "We act, Hashem accomplishes." Surely we must do our best, but our efforts will bear fruit only if Hashem wills it.

May we all merit His mercy.

In Summary

- Remember your child is a sacred trust.
- Avoid overreaction and confrontation.
- If you react with emotion, make sure that your mind is still in control of your feelings.

Afterword

I believe that one of the most important phrases in the Siddur is "אלוקי נשמה שנתת בי טהורה היא." "My G-d, the soul which You have placed in me is pure."

Every Jew possesses a soul imbued with a deep, indelible purity. No matter how many discipline problems you have faced and no matter how long these problems have endured, there is always the chance, no, *likelihood* that you can turn things around.

I would not want to end this book leaving you with a feeling of hopelessness, thinking, "If only I had been told this years ago." You and your children have all the latent potential and *kedusha* which every member of *Klall Yisroel* possesses.

I also believe that the most important value which parents can impart to their children is the knowledge that no person is ever alone. Every Jew not only possesses the merit of Avrohom, Yitzchok and Yaakov, but Hashem remembers the sacrifice of countless generations who placed their belief in Torah-true Judaism above all else. They endured ridicule, poverty, exile, torture and death rather than forget the Covenant that their ancestors entered into at Sinai. These generations stand before Hashem in all of their grandeur and their merit is never forgotten by Him.[1] There is no doubt that Hashem will extend His *siyata dishmaya* to any parent who is continuting to imbue his/her child with a Torah-true *chinuch*.

It is *never too late* to begin the steps which will help fulfill the words of the prophet, "And he will bring back the hearts of fathers through the children and the hearts of children through the fathers (Malachi 3:23)."

---

1. Converts to Judaism are considered to be long-lost relatives. See *Ohr HaChayim*, Devorim 21:11, for a beautiful explanation of the relationship of the soul of a convert vis-à-vis the rest of the Jewish people.

Glossary

Abba: Father

Alter: (Yid.) Literally, "aged one," but used as a title implying reverence.

Avrohom Ovinu: (The Patriarch) Avrohom.

Chazal: Abbreviation for *Chachomeinu Zichronum Livrocha* "Our Sages of blessed memory." This phrase refers to the Sages of the Mishna and Talmud.

Chinuch: Education.

Cholent: A hot dish, prepared before Shabbos, and customarily eaten at the Shabbos midday meal.

Daas Torah: The Torah opinion, or outlook or the religious Jewish perspective, on a given subject.

Gemora: The Talmud.

HaRav HaGaon: An exceptionally learned Torah scholar.

Hashkafa: The Torah philosophy on at a given subject.

Ima: Mother

Kedusha: Sanctity.
Klal Yisroel: The Jewish nation

Maggid: An orator who travels from town to town, exhorting the people to improve their ways.
Mashgiach: The spiritual mentor in a yeshiva.
Mechanech: educator.
Melamed: teacher of the young.

Neshoma (os): Soul(s).

o"h: *olov hasholom* or *oleha hasholom*, abbrevation for "May he/she rest in peace."

Ribono Shel Olom: Master of the World.
Rishonim: The Earlier Masters, representing the period of Torah leaders spanning the Eleventh through Fifteenth Centuries, C.E.
Rosh Yeshiva: Dean of a yeshiva.

Shechina: The Divine Presence.
shlita: Abbreviation for *Sheyichye Leorech Yomim Tovim Amein* — "May he live a long and good life."
Shulchan Oruch: Code of Jewish Law, written by Rav Yosef Karo, *zt"l*, (1488-1575).
Shlomo HaMelech: King Solomon.

zt"l: Abbreviation for *zecher tzaddik livrocho* — "may the memory of the righteous be for a blessing."

Dedicated in Memory of my Beloved Mother

Esther Goldberg

אסתר יעטע בת יעקב ע"ה
כ"ב מנחם-אב, תשנ"ב

She raised me with love,
encouragement, and compassion,
providing a fertile field
for the seeds of Torah
to grow.

May my efforts in spreading Torah
be a source of comfort
to her soul.

ת.נ.צ.ב.ה.

Rabbi Shlomo Goldberg
Venice, California

לזכר נשמת
הורינו

ר' נפתלי בן יעקב זעלענגוט
מרת מלכה בת אלתר חיים
זכרונם לברכה

ר' זאב אריה בן שמעון
מרת ריזל בת צבי הירש הלוי
זכרונם לברכה

שמסרו נפשם על חינוך הבנים והבנות
ת.נ.צ.ב.ה.

לעילוי נשמת
דבורה רייזא בת אשר
Westerman
כ"א סיון תשכ"ז

ולעילוי נשמת
דוד אייזק בן מאיר
Reich
כ"ד חשון תשכ"ז

₰ ₰ ₰

Dedicated in Honor of

Mr. and Mrs. Sherman and Selma Fabian, עמו"ש

In appreciation of their tremendous dedication and self-sacrifice for our education and upbringing. May they continue to harvest the fruits of their dedication for many years to come.

Yisroel and Masha Reeva Fabian, and Family
Nosson and Sorah Rochel Fabian, and Family
Meir and Chaya Fabian, and Family
Zvi Fabian

In Honor of Our Daughter

Masha Reeva, שתחיה

an Extraordinary
Daughter, Wife and Mother
Whose Dedication to Chinuch is Truly an
Inspiration

May Hashem Grant Her and Rav Yisroel, עמו"ש
Continued Nachas and Hatzlocho

Donald and Sondra Botvinick

Audio Cassettes

The following cassettes are available

in America, by writing to:
Orlowek c/o Freilich
45 Villa St.,
Mount Vernon, NY 10552;

in Israel, by writing to:
Orlowek
P.O.B. 1570,
Jerusalem

The cost is $6 per tape, with each sixth tape free. Add $1.40 handling cost for the first tape and 40 cents for each additional tape. Checks should be made payable to Rabbi Noach Orlowek. Allow 6 weeks for delivery.

1. Shabbos — Our Root/Transition To The Week
2. Appreciating And Utilizing Shabbos
3. How To Ask Important Questions
4. How To Feel On Seder Night
5. Pesach: How To Feel That You Left Egypt
6. The Seder
7. Major Concepts Of Seder Night
8. Haggadah: Workbook For Parents And Teachers
9. Song: Its Essence And Its Connection To Pesach
10. Leaving Egypt Twice — An Important Lesson For Life
11a-d. Iyar — Understanding The Month And Its Role In Preparing For Shavuos (four tapes)
12. Lag B'omer — Understanding The Oral Law
13. Shavuous — Appreciating Torah
14. Shavuous — Learning To Listen
15. Preparing To Stand At Sinai

16. Utilizing Opportunities: The Three Weeks
17. The Second Churban And Edom
18. How To Prepare For Rosh Hashona
19. Hashem Is My Light — On Rosh Hashona
20. Practical Growth Suggestions For Rosh Hashona
21. How To Begin To Prepare For Rosh Hashona
22. Rosh Hashona — Responsibility
23. Character Development — Our Role In Rosh Hashona
24. Erev Rosh Hashona
25. Getting The Most Out Of Purim
26. Purim And Amalek
27. Practical Steps To Teshuva
28a-b. Erev Yom Kippur (two tapes)
29. The Yom Kippur And Succos Connection
30. Where Chessed Begins
31. Entering The Realm Of Shidduchim
32. Dealing With Anger In Others
33. How To Influence Others
34. How To Judge Favorably (דן לכף זכות)
35. Insuring A Closeness To Hashem
36. Being A Parent — The Example Of Yaakov
37. Staying Healthy
38a-h. Classroom Discipline (eight tapes)
39. Avrohom As Our Father
40. Redemption
41. Master Of The World
42. Recognizing The Truth
43. Understanding Hashem's World
44. Understanding Hashem's World
45. Knowing Your Test And Knowing Yourself
46. How Hashem Tests Us — And How To Pass
47. The Most Necessary Ingredient
48. Towards Meaningful Prayer
49. Complimenting And Complementing/ Showing A Shining Face

50. Knowing What You Don't Know
51. The Sense Of Sight: Its Use And Misuse
52. Building Upon Your Feelings
53. Looking And Understanding
54. Nature: A Teacher Of Good Character
55. Your Present Situation: Grow Or Escape, Part 1
56. Your Present Situation: Grow Or Escape, Part 2
    (These two tapes deal with whether persons should invest their energy into coping with a situation, or should exert themselves to leave their situation.)
57. Your Greatest Weakness Is Your Greatest Strength
58. Saying Little Helps You Do Much
59. Saying Little Helps You Do Much
60. Making Decisions
61. Making And Keeping Resolutions
62. The Art Of Wanting
63. Believing In Yourself
64. Appreciation Of HaGaon Rav Simcha Wasserman, zt"l
65. Introduction To Character Improvement (Two Tapes)
66. The Blessing Of Self-knowledge
67. Helping Others Cope With Affliction
68. Keys To Effective Communication
69. Fighting The Overpowering Yetzer (יצר המתגבר)
70. Loneliness vs. Solitude
71a. Coping With Adversity
71b. Helping Others Cope With Adversity
72. Pursuing Happiness
73. Having Eyes In Your Head/How To Achieve And Retain Good Fortune
74a-b. Appreciating Yourself (two tapes)
75. The Dynamics Of Leadership
76. Learning To Be Flexible/Chanukkah: Utilizing Opportunities
77a-b. Reaching Inward vs. Reaching Out (two tapes)
78. What Is Emuna

79. How To Retain Your Learning
80. Emuna — Its Basic Element
81. Bitochon vs. Hishtadlus
82. The How And Why Of Loving Hashem
83. The Shechina Is With Us — Always
84. The Mishkon — Hallmark In Jewish History
85. The Mishkon — A Deeper Understanding Of Avodah
86. Balancing Learning And Doing
87. What's Good (Tov) — What's True (Emes) (Defining Terms)
88a-b. Truth And Stability (two tapes)
89. The Secret Behind Yitzchok's Brocha
90. Attaining Emuna And Bitachon

ORDER FORM

Please send:

Copies of   Tape #   Title

_____   _____   _____
_____   _____   _____
_____   _____   _____
_____   _____   _____
_____   _____   _____
_____   _____   _____

Each tape is $6 with each 6th tape free. Add $1.40 handling for first tape and $ .40 for each additional tape.

_____ tapes _$_____
handling _$_____
total enclosed _$_____

Please ship to:
Name: _____
Street: _____
City: _____ State _____ Zip____